Writing Strategies for Fiction

Author

Jessica Hathaway

Contributing Authors

Stephanie Macceca, M.A.Ed.

Sarah Kartchner Clark, Ph.D.

Publishing Credits

Robin Erickson, *Production Director;* Lee Aucoin, *Creative Director;* Timothy J. Bradley, *Illustration Manager;* Sara Johnson, M.S.Ed., *Editorial Director;* Grace Alba Le, *Designer;* Sandra Canchola, *Editorial Assistant;* Corinne Burton, M.A.Ed., *Publisher*

Image Credits

Cover, p. 1 The Bridgeman Art Library; All other images Shutterstock

Standards

© 2010 National Governors Association Center for Best Practices and Council of Chief State School Officers (CCSS)
© 2004 Mid-continent Research for Education and Learning (McREL)
© 2007 Teachers of English to Speakers of Other Languages, Inc. (TESOL)
© 2007 Board of Regents of the University of Wisconsin System. World-Class Instructional Design and Assessment (WIDA). For more information on using the WIDA ELP Standards, please visit the WIDA website at www.wida.us.

Shell Education

5301 Oceanus Drive
Huntington Beach, CA 92649-1030
http://www.shelleducation.com
ISBN 978-1-4258-1006-1
© 2014 Shell Education Publishing, Inc.

Table of Contents

Table of Contents *(cont.)*

What Is Writing?

For thousands of years, humans have been communicating by writing down characters, symbols, numbers, or letters with implied meaning. Being able to write and to write well is more important today than ever before, given the complex world in which we live. Writing is the making of letters or characters that constitute readable matter with the intent to convey meaning. Writing demands that one not only knows how to read what one has written but also knows the rules of writing that dictate how characters or letters are to be written and therefore understood.

What is writing? Is it brainstorming? Is it spelling? Is it scribbling words and phrases? Is it a report? Is it a simple paragraph? Writing in the classroom can be simply defined as any symbolic representation (Hefflin and Hartman 2002). As Bena Hefflin and Douglas Hartman explain, the definition of writing includes representations that are "linguistic, graphic, pictorial, or otherwise." This broad definition of writing welcomes a wide variety of writing formats.

Everyone Should Teach Writing

Because educators understand the need for improved reading and writing skills in students, there has been a renewed focus on teaching literacy skills within the Common Core State Standards (National Governors Association Center for Best Practices, Council of Chief State School Officers 2010). Furthermore, there is also an increased emphasis on the shared responsibility of teachers across disciplines and content areas to help students develop the necessary reading and writing skills to succeed in that particular subject. Pam Allyn supports this claim, making her argument for the shared responsibility of teachers to teach literacy skills as she closely analyzes the word *core* itself, noting that "the word *core* is a homonym: *core* and *corps*…[The Common Core] is at once about the *core* of why you teach and how you can enhance every aspect of your work…[It] is also about building a true *corps* of teachers, parents, and communities working together to ensure that *every* child has the certainty of gaining college- and career-ready outcomes," shifting the responsibility from a single classroom teacher to a body of teachers, parents, and community members who are collectively responsible for ensuring the academic success of the children in their community (Allyn 2013, 4–5).

Because of curriculum demands, many teachers feel there is not enough time to teach writing; adding one more component is just too much strain on the time and quality of lessons. However, researchers claim that most writing assignments do not need to be graded, which eliminates a major concern about the teacher workload (Worsley and Mayer 1989; Hightshue et al. 1988; Self 1987). And writing assignments can serve as ongoing assessments of students' understanding of fictional texts, which informs future instruction and helps "teachers determine what students need and then design an appropriate instructional response" (Harvey 1998, 203). In this sense, writing instruction in any classroom cannot be overlooked as it is a powerful tool for assessing both students' understanding of fiction texts and the traits of good writing.

Writing is an instrument of thinking that allows students to express their thoughts and helps them understand and share their perceptions of the world around them. Teachers can give students power in their world by teaching them to write and to write well. The written word "enables the writer, perhaps for the first time, to sense the power of . . . language to affect another. Through using, selecting and rejecting, arranging and rearranging language, the student comes to understand how language is used" (Greenberg and Rath 1985, 12).

What Is Writing? *(cont.)*

Literacy Demands

The literacy needs for the 21st century are tremendous. Literacy was defined a century ago as one's ability to write one's name. A literate person could write his or her name; an illiterate person could not. In 1940, more than "half of the U.S. population had completed no more than an eighth grade education," which is an evolving statistic as education continues to change and develop into the 21st century (National Center for Education Statistics 2013).

Education as an institution is similarly evolving to meet the demands of what it means to be considered literate in the 21st century. With the advent of the Common Core State Standards (National Governors Association Center for Best Practices, Council of Chief State School Officers 2010), students are considered literate individuals when:

1. They demonstrate independence.

2. They build strong content knowledge.

3. They respond to the varying demands of audience, task, purpose, and discipline.

4. They comprehend as well as critique.

5. They value evidence.

6. They use technology and digital media strategically and capably.

7. They come to understand other perspectives and cultures.

Furthermore, students who meet the standards outlined in the Common Core State Standards by the time they leave high school are "prepared to enter college and workforce training programs" with success (National Governors Association Center for Best Practices, Council of Chief State School Officers 2010). There is a clear movement toward fostering the skills necessary for students to succeed in real-world contexts and thrive as productive citizens and workers. This need to develop productive members of the workforce is in line with alarming findings related to dropout rates and the U.S. economy (Wolk 2011, 75):

> *An analysis by the Alliance for Excellent Education (2010) shows that the U.S. economy would grow significantly if the number of high school dropouts were cut in half. If just half of these students had graduated, research shows, they would have generated more than $4.1 billion in additional earning every year, and states and localities would have received additional taxes of more than $535 million. If the nation continues to lose students at the present rate, about 13 million students will drop out in the next 10 years at a financial loss of $3 trillion (Alliance for Excellent Education, 2009).*

What Is Writing? *(cont.)*

The cost of high school dropouts to the economy is clear, and the impact of this unfortunate statistic should not be ignored in the midst of today's economic state. But what can classroom teachers do to remedy these findings? Why are students dropping out of high school at such an alarming rate? Does the desire to drop out begin in high school or long before? Research suggests that the reasons behind student-dropout rates take root long before students make the active choice to drop out. In fact, experts in the field claim that to make a lasting difference in high school dropout rates, "we must understand and focus on why students choose to leave school. Dropping out is not an impulsive decision. The process begins long before high school, often by the 4th or 5th grade. More often than not *it is rooted in the failure of students to learn to read*—not just decode the English language, but to read and understand what they read" (Wolk 2011, 77; italics added). Teachers need to develop in students the *desire* to read, to actively read, to habitually read, and to read with comprehension and purpose. When students read an extensive amount of literature and informational texts, they absorb the variety of language being used and can apply it to their written work. Students are experiencing failure in reading at an early age, which significantly impacts their motivation to read, write, and develop the skills necessary to be considered college and career ready. We must examine how to effectively motivate students to read and write and instill the lifelong love for reading that goes hand in hand with reading independence, comprehension, and deep learning expressed through writing. But to understand how to instill this thirst for reading and writing, teachers must first understand *who* their students are and how the learning needs of these 21st-century students differ from previous generations during a time when technology and digital learning played a small role in students' lives both in and out of the classroom.

Technology and 21st-Century Learning

It is no secret that technology is drastically changing education and, consequently, the lives of young people growing up in the "Net Generation." As such, what it means to be literate in the context of advanced technology is not the same definition from even a decade ago. In "Comprehending and Learning From Internet Sources: Processing Patterns of Better and Poorer Learners," Susan Goldman et al. (2012) noted that technology is "changing the face of literacy," stating that people of all ages look to the Internet to resolve a variety of problems that "arise in academic, personal, interpersonal, and occupational contexts" (356–357). Students are looking to the Web for their schoolwork, which makes the development of 21st-century skills crucial to students' ability to strategically navigate and "critically evaluate information sources for their relevance, reliability, and consistency," as nearly anyone can post information—regardless of its validity—to the Internet.

Having said that, it is no wonder that the strategic use and navigation of technology and digital media is included in the Common Core State Standards definition of literacy in the 21st century. Students must learn to integrate and evaluate the information they encounter on a daily basis from diverse media, including both print and digital resources, whether in school or at home. We have entered a new era in education, and this era is deeply tied to the technological advances that now permeate our modern lives. Today, children can use a cell phone to take a picture before they can speak. A typical three-year-old can turn on a computer and begin a game program without assistance from an adult. Students in school can use the Internet and online libraries to access information from remote locations. They can interview experts in faraway locations through email.

What Is Writing? (cont.)

According to Susan Metros, Professor of Clinical Education at the University of Southern California, college students today are "media-stimulated, but not necessarily media-literate" (quoted in Wagner 2008, 183–184). But today's college students are not the same learners who are presently immersed in today's elementary and secondary education system. Bearing this in mind, the Common Core State Standards emphasize the development of those skills in preparation for college and careers beyond the classroom. The hope is that students become media-literate as they meet the standards outlined in the Common Core and are able to navigate the complexities of the digital realm. Now more than ever, it is each teacher's responsibility and duty to prepare students for the reading and writing demands of our technological age. In order to become effective and efficient readers and writers, students need to use comprehension strategies automatically and independently. Students need teacher guidance to help them become independent readers, writers, and learners so that they not only understand what they read but can question it and write about it.

The Reading/Writing Connection

According to Gay Su Pinnell (1988), "as children read and write they make the connections that form their basic understandings about both. Learning in one area enhances learning in the other. There is ample evidence to suggest that the processes are inseparable and that we should examine pedagogy in the light of these interrelationships. Hence, the two activities should be integrated in instructional settings. Teachers need to create supportive situations in which children have opportunities to explore the whole range of literacy learning, and they need to design instruction that helps children make connections between reading and writing." Additionally, "a considerable mismatch between reading phases and writing phases is a red flag to indicate that instruction is not balanced," so providing students with opportunities to read and write will help to remedy this imbalance and work toward building students' overall literacy skills (Gentry 2006, 35). Moreover, J. Richard Gentry goes on to say that "children who receive little opportunity to write in school…and too little appropriate writing instruction sometimes excel as readers but struggle as writers and spellers" (35).

Writing is the expression of ideas and thoughts gathered while reading. Fictional texts are often heavily loaded with difficult vocabulary words and complex concepts that are challenging for students to understand. Encouraging students to both read and write about fiction helps them understand, for example, the themes, characters, and plots within a given fictional text as they synthesize and express their understanding through writing. When students read fictional texts without writing about it, they miss a crucial step in the process of understanding the text because "writing serves as a vehicle for learning both content standards and standards of written expression" (Combs 2012, 12).

The connection between reading and writing is complex and intricate, placing the act of reading as a necessary and crucial counterpart to writing: "Reading cannot be separated from writing. It's neither research-based, practicable, nor sensible to read first without writing. Students must connect reading and writing everyday (Routman 2004). It has to be writing *and* reading first" (Gentry 2006, 145). In fact, this notion is especially true for young writers as nearly "half of the time that beginning readers invest in a piece of writing is spent on reading rather than writing. Many children reread multiple times as they write

Motivating Students to Write (cont.)

Teachers can create a fiction library corner in their classroom libraries by collecting and providing high-interest fictional texts for students to read in addition to expository writing about fiction (e.g., essays, book reports, literary analyses) that will serve as good models for writing *about* fiction. Teachers have an intimate knowledge of fiction-based reading materials for a wide range of reading abilities, so they can recommend books to any student to read outside of class.

Lesley Mandel Morrow, president of the International Reading Association (2003–04), explains that research indicates children in classrooms with literature collections read 50 percent more books than children in classrooms without such collections. As such, this percentage likely translates into the sheer volume of writing students are able to produce. Students synthesize themes, character development, and other elements of fiction through expository (nonfiction) pieces (Morrow 1996). According to Harvey (1998, 4), "the best nonfiction writing emerges from topics the writer knows, cares, and wonders about and wants to pursue," which makes the availability of expository and other nonfiction writing about fictional texts critical to the development of students' ability to express their understanding of the themes and concepts through writing. Students need to read many literary analyses and formal essays in order to know what good expository writing is. With the availability of high-interest texts, students are able to identify their interests and pursue topics that they find highly engaging to write about.

High-Interest Texts

Working with the school librarian or media specialist and parent organizations is a great way to build a sizeable collection of texts for their classrooms, which can be a mixture of informational and fictional books from which students can choose to read based on their interests. Bear in mind that this library may serve to generate the interest to read and write about a variety of texts on many different subjects, so providing students with a wide range of texts from which to choose will be beneficial in fostering students' desire and motivation to read and write. In addition to simply providing students with informational and fictional texts, be sure to provide texts that are at your students' readiness levels and also those that may present more of a challenge. The rich diversity of language students will encounter from immersing themselves in high-interest texts will serve as models of good writing around which students can mirror their own writing about fiction, allowing them to express their understanding and comprehension of thematic connections and other fictional topics coherently and purposefully. Especially with interest-based texts, students can build their prior knowledge about a given topic at a less challenging reading level, in turn preparing them to apply their understanding through writing. "Michael Pressley and his colleagues (2003) . . . found high-motivational and high-performing classrooms were, above all, filled with books at different levels of text difficulty. Conversely, on their list of the characteristics of classroom practices that undermine motivation and achievement is: 'The teacher does not give students opportunities to have power over their own learning. Students do not have choice in their work'" (Calkins, Ehrenworth, and Lehman 2012, 50), which is counterproductive to what we as teachers aim to achieve in the context of the Common Core: fostering the literacy skills students need to be "college and career ready." Furthermore, according to Fink (2006, 79), "the more a student reads in one content area, the 'richer' or better that student's reading becomes in that content area," which in turn will translate into students' success with writing about fictional texts—as students absorb the academic language of expository (nonfiction) texts about fiction, they can apply this language to their own formal writing pieces

Motivating Students to Write *(cont.)*

about different works of literature. This notion is in line with Fink's other findings regarding the language acquisition of English language learners, which is applicable to all students' language acquisition: "To encourage striving readers . . . to read [and write] about their interests, teachers should create their own content area libraries full of enticing materials at all readability levels" (81).

Often, students are unaware they have interest in particular genres or authors, for example, until they encounter them for the first time, so providing a variety of texts written by many authors, genres, and topics can only serve to offer students a wide variety of texts from which to read and write about. Additionally, research suggests that the most influential factor in motivating students to read is "ensuring the students [have] easy access to high-interest texts," so making these high-interest texts available to your students is an important factor to consider when developing your classroom library (Calkins, Ehrenworth, and Lehman 2012, 50). To support students' writing, it is important to provide them with a variety of high-interest reading materials—both fictional texts and informational texts *about* fiction—that both motivate and inspire them throughout the writing process. Fictional literature covers a wide range of topics, styles, and themes, and the types of fiction that interest one reader may not interest another. Therefore, it is important to provide an assortment of different types of fiction that can appeal to different types of students. The following categories represent several main types of fiction that can interest and motivate a variety of students:

- Science Fiction (e.g., *The Magic School Bus* books by Joanna Cole and *The Hunger Games* by Suzanne Collins)
- Historical Fiction (e.g., *Little House on the Prairie* by Laura Ingalls Wilder and *The Midwife's Apprentice* by Karen Cushman)
- Mystery (e.g., *Chasing Vermeer* series by Blue Balliet and *The Westing Game* by Ellen Raskin)
- Fantasy (e.g., the *Harry Potter* series by J.K. Rowling and *Ella Enchanted* by Gail Carson Levine)
- Adventure (e.g., *Heroes of Olympus* by Rick Riordan and *Hatchet* by Gary Paulsen)

Differentiation

In addition to building motivation through interest-based texts, below-level students will benefit from scaffolding as well. They may need to be constantly reminded to refer to their rubric—which should be adapted to address their individual needs—to meet the expectations of the assignment. Teachers can provide graphic organizers during the prewriting phase to help these students get started in an organized fashion. When revising and editing, teachers can model how to identify errors and make changes so that these students have a clear understanding of this difficult stage of the writing process.

Above-level students can be challenged at each step of the writing process to work more independently, create longer or more elaborate pieces, use multiple sources, write from different points of view, incorporate richer vocabulary, or write with a greater variety of sentence structures. Teachers should also adapt rubrics to challenge these students.

The English language learner should not be left out of this discussion. Second language acquisition for English language learners is strikingly similar for native English speakers and non-native English

Motivating Students to Write (cont.)

speakers: "*English reading and writing development processes are essentially similar for both English learners and native English speakers…*That is, in reading, all learners gradually come to use their developing English language knowledge, their world knowledge, and their understanding of print conventions to make sense of written text. Similarly, in writing, they use their developing English language knowledge, world knowledge, and understanding of print conventions to put their ideas on paper" (Peregoy and Boyle 2005, 159). In looking at this statement, it is clear that the relationship between reading and writing is not exclusively reserved for native English speakers; language acquisition—whether first or second language acquisition—is largely similar for all students, so the explicit instruction of both reading *and* writing strategies will help to remedy any imbalances in reading and writing skills you identify in your English language learners.

The demographics of students in our classrooms today is becoming increasingly more diverse, prompting teachers to differentiate their instruction to allow for students of all backgrounds and languages to develop the skills necessary to succeed. And with this growing diversity, it is important to note that English language learners often struggle with more than just accessing content but also with developing literacy skills in the context of unfamiliar cultural references, tales, and legends that native English speakers are naturally more familiar with. Because the Common Core State Standards emphasize the shared responsibility of teachers to help students learn to comprehend and write critically, providing English language learners with access to texts that will help develop their overall reading ability is also essential to developing their writing skills. English language learners "will benefit from actively seeking exposure to language and social interaction with others who can provide meaningful input in the second language. Furthermore, they—and you, the teacher—can enhance students' English language skills by placing language learning in meaningful and interesting contexts" (Dunlap and Weisman 2006, 11).

It is our responsibility to provide students with meaningful and interesting contexts to learn language and build their literacy skills. The ability to synthesize the many aspects of fiction and demonstrate mastery of particular skills and knowledge through writing hinges on each student's ability to dissect and interact with texts, unquestionably marking the act of reading as a necessary skill to succeed with academic writing. When implementing the writing strategies in this book, discuss the importance of using a variety of writing strategies to express their understanding of the fictional trends and themes they observe from their reading of fictional texts so that the importance of reading, writing, and developing fine-tuned literacy skills is effectively communicated and made known. The explicit instruction of the writing strategies provides English language learners with meaningful contexts for learning language, so this discussion is of the utmost importance in establishing a reason for writing about fiction, not only for your English language learners but for all of your students. In doing so, teachers simultaneously aid in the development of students' collaborative, communicative, and group-based skills emphasized in the Common Core State Standards' Speaking & Listening skills, subsequently helping all students to strategically communicate and interact with those around them within the context of the English language.

The Writing Process

"A writer," say Britton et al. (1975, 47), "draws on the whole store of his experience, and his whole social being, so that in the act of writing he imposes his own individuality." The most complex form of writing is the college-level argumentative essay. Taking notes is the least complex form of writing. Writing for meaning and expressing oneself to others is intricate and complex work. Using the writing process helps the writer take a piece of writing from the beginning, or brainstorming, to the end, or the published piece. This process is especially important to follow as students write reports, essays, and other writing assignments. The writing process at the emergent writing level is usually conducted as a group, though on occasion it is done individually. Students in higher grades who have more familiarity with the writing process can complete it individually.

What is the writing process? It includes prewriting, drafting, revising/editing, publishing, and reflection. Read the description of the writing process steps below. There are different points to consider at each step of the writing process.

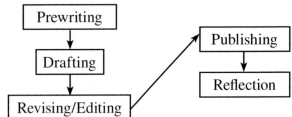

Prewriting

This is the phase during which all writing begins. At this stage, writers generate ideas, brainstorm topics, web ideas together, or talk and think about ideas. Teachers explain that students may get writing ideas from personal experiences, stories, pictures, magazines, newspapers, television, and a variety of other sources.

This phase sets the foundation for a specific piece of writing. Before brainstorming or prewriting can begin, students need instruction on the genre or format (research report, journal entry, visual presentation, etc.), audience (the teacher, fellow classmates, their families, editors of the school magazine, etc.), and purpose (to explain, to persuade, to inform, etc.). These elements impact the types of information to brainstorm.

Students need to have a clear understanding of a writing assignment (i.e., the prompt) before they are expected to write or report on it. Teachers can provide resources for research and model note-taking strategies. Essay prompts and other writing assignments that require deep textual analysis or synthesizing major themes are often complex and difficult to understand, so discussion will help prepare students to write. Such strategies as Note-Taking (pages 118–132) and Using Diagrams and Maps (pages 133–161) can help students organize the major points in their writing.

What does prewriting look like?

- researching a chosen topic, using print and digital sources
- analyzing the characteristics of the intended genre
- examining sample writing pieces
- discussing the topic with the teacher, a partner, or the class
- brainstorming ideas about the topic
- using webbing or other graphics to organize information
- discussing the assessment tool

Writing About Fiction (cont.)

Rubrics

Students' writing should be formally assessed at the end of the writing process as students submit final, polished pieces that demonstrate their understanding of concepts and topics related to fiction. Providing students with straightforward rubrics that clearly lay out your expectations is effective in sharing which components of students' writing will be evaluated and each component's quantifiable importance. In doing so, you inform students which pieces of their writing hold the greatest significance for that particular assignment and which skills they should focus on most. However, in order to create a well-crafted rubric, you must first identify the learning objectives of the assignment and how much weight to give to each component on the rubric.

Consider evaluating students' mastery of content knowledge and students' writing skills in different categories, allowing for you to both evaluate how well they understand the concept being investigated through writing and how well they articulate their understanding through their written work. As appropriate to the assignment, assign each category (e.g., Ideas, Audience, Structure, Thematic Understanding) a quantifiable value (e.g., 1–10 or A–F) that students understand and skills that students are prepared to demonstrate (e.g., *Strong audience awareness; Engages the reader throughout*). Distribute rubrics to students to support them as they set out to begin a writing task, continuing to refer to your expectations throughout the writing process as they work toward completing the assignment. This way, you reiterate your expectations and support students' growth as writers in a very clear and straightforward manner in which skills and expectations are both attainable and quantifiable.

Informal Feedback

After distributing rubrics and thoroughly discussing your expectations for a particular assignment, confer with your student writers during the writing process to provide them with an informal setting to workshop their writing and to improve their written communication prior to evaluating their final work.

Conferring

Conferring with students is a form of assessment that is interactive, and the immediacy of your verbal feedback is invaluable to students' development as writers. Ask students about their work, their ideas, their understanding of fiction-related concepts, and their grasp of the conventions of writing, among other questions. Model for students the best strategies for editing and revising their work. Whether conferring with students individually or in small groups, constructively critique students' writing by acknowledging areas in which students have met or are working toward meeting your expectations and areas that need improvement, being mindful to not overload students with excessive, unfocused comments. Your informal feedback should guide students in the direction of meeting the criteria for the assignment but not to the point where revising their work seems like an impossible task. Allow students to maintain ownership of their work by suggesting "options or open-ended alternatives students can choose for their revision path" (University of Nebraska–Lincoln Writing Center 2013). In doing so, students learn both to assess their own writing and to revise accordingly. Conferring with the young writers in your classroom is crucial to their development and growth as writers.

Writing About Fiction *(cont.)*

Written Comments

As students work toward meeting the expectations for a particular writing assignment, reviewing their drafts and providing them with specific and focused feedback is vital to their success in conveying their fictional knowledge through writing. When reviewing students' drafts, making notes on their work may prove effective in identifying specific areas in need of improvement (e.g., marking misspelled words, grammatical errors, or unclear and unfinished thoughts). Identifying these areas of improvement will inform your instruction, allowing you to modify your explicit teaching of the writing strategies in order to help students become better writers. Apart from specific feedback, you can evaluate the written work as a whole (e.g., writing comments at the end of a paper), with less focus on particulars and more emphasis on the overall success of the written piece in meeting the expectations identified in the rubric.

Spotlight Reading

Providing students with informal feedback can be an enjoyable moment, as well, one in which students are excited to share their work with the class. Set aside a time each week for students to read aloud and share the writing they have accomplished or are working on. These writings may be less formal pieces such as journals, free writes, or feature analyses, or they may be formal writing pieces like essays. This practice keeps students focused and aware of an audience as they write, and it allows them the opportunity to give and receive feedback. It is an effective way to validate the hard work and effort of students and may even eliminate the need for the teacher to formally assess a piece of writing. Finally, this spotlight reading also provides an opportunity for students to hear their writing aloud. They will automatically think of things they are learning about, and they will become more aware of what they need to change to improve their writing.

Writing Instruction

What Great Teachers Do to Encourage Writing

1. **Share vocabulary-rich books and reading materials about the subjects you are studying in class.** Megan Sloan (1996) explains that the best source of learning about vocabulary is reading good books that use the words. This allows the teacher to introduce them, allows the opportunity for students to hear them in context, and provides an opportunity to discuss the vocabulary words.

2. **Provide plenty of time for students to experience the writing process** (Corona, Spangenberger, and Venet 1998). It takes time to teach the writing process, but it is worth it. Taking a writing project from planning to publication is very meaningful to students because it validates their efforts and understanding of fiction-related concepts.

3. **Allow time for students to evaluate others' writing and receive teacher feedback** (Corona, Spangenberger, and Venet 1998). Writing is communication. Students need to share their writing with others, both giving and receiving feedback from peers and teachers. This helps to cement students' understanding of fiction-related concepts. The process also provides teachers with the opportunity to clarify and reteach concepts as needed.

4. **Offer daily writing opportunities to your students.** "A writer-centered classroom emphasizes using written expression to communicate ideas. Writing is an important part of all areas of the curriculum" (Corona, Spangenberger, and Venet 1998, 29). Be sure to include a wide variety of assignments. Some assignments might be more formal, while others may be more casual. Also include a range of different types of writing such as journal entries, outlines, poetry, reports, and short stories. Students usually benefit from having a choice regarding what they are asked to write about. Encourage students to use relevant vocabulary when they write.

5. **Encourage students to be aware of and look for new and interesting words.** Students can browse through books looking for words that catch their attention and add them to their vocabulary journals. They may also be assigned to look for specific words that are being studied in class. Finally, create a Word Wall in your classroom (see pages 34–37).

6. **Incorporate practice and repetition as a way for students to become familiar with vocabulary words and how they are to be used** (Laflamme 1997). Students can be exposed through writing, discussions, modeling, classroom exercises, and reading.

7. **Teach students the strategies to read, understand, and write about increasingly complex text.** These same strategies can help students work through difficult concepts to arrive at deep learning. Students who can recognize text patterns will be better prepared to use those patterns in their own writing (Fisher and Ivey 2005).

8. **Focus students' reading and writing on big ideas. Don't get caught up in the details.** Rote learning does not lend itself to lifelong learning. Focusing on themes, concepts, and big ideas lends itself to linking new information to prior knowledge as well as life experiences and events that are happening in the world today.

Writing Instruction (cont.)

Writing Venues in Your Classroom

There are a variety of ways to teach students new ideas and to incorporate writing into the curriculum. Teachers often lecture to the whole class and seldom pair students or assign small groups to work together for reading and writing. Following are suggestions for the types of configurations any teacher can consider:

Large groups are best for:

- introducing a new writing strategy
- modeling think-alouds to show how good writers work through a piece of writing
- practicing think-alouds to apply a strategy to students' own writing and allowing students to share their experiences and ideas using the strategy

Small groups are best for:

- providing more intensive instruction for students who need it
- introducing above-level students to a new writing piece or strategy so that they can apply it independently to more challenging writing assignments
- preteaching new strategies and vocabulary to English language learners or below-level students

Conferences are best for:

- checking students' understanding of fiction-related concepts and the writing strategies being used
- providing intensive writing strategy instruction for students who may need extra attention
- coaching students in how they might reveal their thinking by writing to others
- pushing students to use a strategy to think more deeply than they might have imagined possible
- individually editing and correcting student writing

Pair students with partners:

- to discuss free writes, dialogue journals, think-pair-share, etc.
- to edit and gather input on product writing pieces

Habits of Highly Effective Writers

Nell Duke and P. David Pearson (2001) have established that good readers read and write a lot. They also set goals, make predictions, and read selectively. Many of the same practices of good readers are also done by good writers. Here are some more specific suggestions for highly effective writers:

- Good writers write all the time. The more experience one has writing, the better writer he or she becomes. Learning to write takes practice and more practice!
- Good writers read a lot. Reading provides a great model for writers as to what the finished product looks like (Fisher and Ivey 2005). Students who read will know how to write better than those who do not.

Writing Instruction (cont.)

- Good writers are aware of correct spelling. There are no excuses for poor spelling. Commit to learning and using correct spelling in writing—even in the rough draft, if possible. Good writers use all the resources available and understand the limitations of computer spell-check programs.

- Good writers appreciate critiques and feedback. Good writers have a "thick skin" and ask for input and suggestions from many different sources.

- Good writers keep a learning log handy. The learning log can be used to store good writing ideas, to document what is being learned, to activate prior knowledge, and to question what is being learned (Brozo and Simpson 2003; Fisher and Frey 2004). Using this learning log also helps cement learning and helps students avoid writer's block.

- Good writers write for a variety of purposes. Learning to write in a variety of formats makes for a well-rounded, experienced writer. Teachers should expose students to different types of writing formats for examining fictional texts.

- Good writers read and edit other people's writing. Good writers look for opportunities to work with others to improve their writing. Peer editing groups are an excellent way to get feedback and reinforcement from peers. This feedback is important for the self-image of the writer (Gahn 1989). Editing others' work will also help students recognize writing errors, such as an off-topic response, a weak topic sentence, a lack of supporting detail, weak vocabulary, and errors in spelling or grammar.

- Good writers think objectively. Good writers need to be able to step back and really look at their writing. Some writers are so eager to be done with their writing that they never really look at it again.

- Good writers read it out loud! Teachers can encourage students to give their writing a voice. Many errors or additions are discovered when a student listens to the writing being read aloud.

- Good writers use and create rubrics and checklists. Mary Huba and Jann Freed (2000) reiterate the importance of using and creating rubrics and checklists, which help to clarify the expectations for writing assignments. Rubrics and checklists also enable students to become self-directed in mastering the content learning.

How to Use This Book

The focus of this research-based book is to demonstrate how to incorporate more writing into your classroom. Increasing the use of writing is a key way to promote stronger literacy in students. Research shows that using writing is the best way to help students understand the complex concepts and terms introduced in fictional texts. This book provides teachers with the information needed to implement writing activities and assignments that correlate with objectives and goals. The strong research connection in this book helps tie together what teachers actually do in the classroom with the most current research available.

Each section opens with an overview of research in that area to emphasize the importance of that particular writing strategy. Following each skill overview is a variety of instructional writing strategies to improve students' written abilities. Each strategy includes a description and the purpose of the strategy and the research basis. Following the strategy descriptions are grade-level examples of how the strategy applies to fiction. The grade level spans for which the strategy is most appropriate (1–2, 3–5, 6–8, or 9–12) and the language arts standards that are addressed are included. Suggestions for differentiating instruction are provided for English language learners, below- and above-level students. A blank template of the activity sheet is included as a reproducible where applicable as well as on the accompanying Digital Resource CD. Reproducibles are available on the Digital Resource CD in PDF form and often as Word documents to allow for customization of content and text for students of diverse abilities and needs.

Part 1: Writing to Learn

This section is composed of strategies for using writing to learn in the context of fictional texts. These include developing vocabulary, previewing and reviewing, journal writing, note-taking, and using diagrams and maps. These strategies use writing as a tool for students to process and personalize what they learn so that they are able to synthesize and break down the complex fictional characteristics and concepts.

Part 2: Writing to Apply

This section offers strategies for using writing to apply new knowledge: authoring, summarizing, and applying knowledge in all genres. These strategies provide opportunities to utilize the entire writing process to compose a piece of writing that incorporates their knowledge of fiction-related concepts. Teachers may wish to use strategies from Part 1 as building blocks for working toward these application assignments.

Part 3: Assessing Writing

This section describes several holistic assessment options for writing. Each strategy listed in the book includes the purpose for and benefits of the strategy and its connection to writing and fiction, the grade levels for which it is appropriate, and the McREL and Common Core standards that it meets. A step-by-step activity description follows, along with variations, if appropriate, and differentiated instruction to accommodate all types of students. These alterations and suggestions are written for English language learners, above-level students, and students who are reading and writing below grade level.

Correlation to Standards

Shell Education is committed to producing educational materials that are research and standards based. In this effort, we have correlated all of our products to the academic standards of all 50 United States, the District of Columbia, the Department of Defense Dependents Schools, and all Canadian provinces and territories.

How to Find Standards Correlations

To print a customized correlation report of this product for your state, visit our website at **http://www.shelleducation.com** and follow the on-screen directions. If you require assistance in printing correlation reports, please contact Customer Service at **1-877-777-3450**.

Purpose and Intent of Standards

Legislation mandates that all states adopt academic standards that identify the skills students will learn in kindergarten through grade twelve. Many states also have standards for Pre–K. This same legislation sets requirements to ensure the standards are detailed and comprehensive.

Standards are designed to focus instruction and guide adoption of curricula. Standards are statements that describe the criteria necessary for students to meet specific academic goals. They define the knowledge, skills, and content students should acquire at each level. Standards are also used to develop standardized tests to evaluate students' academic progress. Teachers are required to demonstrate how their lessons meet state standards. State standards are used in the development of all of our products, so educators can be assured they meet the academic requirements of each state.

Common Core State Standards

The lessons in this book are aligned to the Common Core State Standards (CCSS). The standards support the objectives presented throughout the lessons and are provided on the Digital Resource CD (standards.pdf).

McREL Compendium

We use the Mid-continent Research for Education and Learning (McREL) Compendium to create standards correlations. Each year, McREL analyzes state standards and revises the compendium. By following this procedure, McREL is able to produce a general compilation of national standards. Each lesson in this product is based on one or more McREL standards, which are provided on the Digital Resource CD (standards.pdf).

TESOL and WIDA Standards

The lessons in this book promote English language development for English language learners. The standards correlations can be found on the Digital Resource CD (standards.pdf).

Correlation to Standards (cont.)

The main focus of the strategies presented in this book is to promote the implementation of explicit writing instruction about fictional texts. The correlating standards for the strategies in this resource are provided on the Digital Resource CD (standards.pdf).

Common Core State Standards

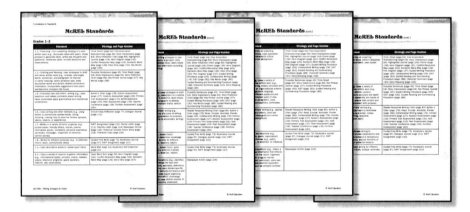

McREL Standards

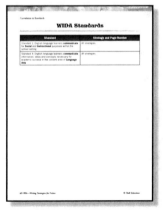

TESOL and WIDA Standards

Developing Vocabulary Overview

Vocabulary and Writing

Extensive research shows that the size of a student's vocabulary is directly related to a student's ability to read (Laflamme 1997). The larger the vocabulary, the easier it is for students to read. The connection between vocabulary and writing is even stronger. One's ability to write is directly tied to one's ability to understand and use vocabulary words. Unlike with reading, students do not have the benefit of using context clues to determine the meaning of words. As writers, they are creating the context clues!

Wesley Becker (1977) has determined that the deficiencies a student may have in vocabulary may lead to poor academic achievement. With the pressure to increase the science, technology, and mathematical skills of students, there is no room to fail. Enriching the vocabulary of students is a necessity if we want students to continue to build and learn new concepts.

Because students are exposed to a large number of new vocabulary words in the language arts classroom, they need opportunities to interact with these words to become familiar with them and build them into their background knowledge. Students will not internalize and remember these words by reading alone. They must learn to know and understand these words well enough to write about them. Their writing and comprehension skills depend upon it. According to Cathy Corona, Sandra Spangenberger, and Iris Venet (1998), "at any level, written communication is more effective when a depth of vocabulary and command of language is evident" (26). Research about vocabulary demonstrates the need for an emphasis on writing for students to understand new terms. Writing is the way a student can personalize unfamiliar terms and incorporate them into his or her vocabulary. Students should be engaged in activities during which they discuss and write about new terms and concepts as well as generate questions, predict answers, and evaluate evidence. Building students' vocabulary will assist teachers in accomplishing this task. The following strategies provide teachers with vocabulary exercises and activities to help build students' vocabulary.

So how do students increase their vocabulary in order to incorporate it into their writing? Research suggests that we learn the meaning of words by using them in the context of "old" words we already know and understand (Adams 1990). New learning is continually building on old or previous learning. The same is true for old and new vocabulary words. New vocabulary words are learned by building on known words. We use these "old" words to describe and define new vocabulary. Most of learning is acquired through language (Adams 1990). The learning occurs through accessing prior language and connecting it to new language.

Developing Vocabulary Overview (cont.)

Standards Addressed

The following chart shows the correlating standards for each strategy in this section. Refer to the Digital Resource CD (standards.pdf) to read the correlating standards in their entirety.

Strategy	McREL Standards	Common Core State Standards
Word Wall	Grades 1–2 (2.1) Grades 3–5 (2.1) Grades 6–8 (2.1) Grades 9–12 (2.1)	Grade 1 (L.1.4, L.1.6) Grade 2 (L.2.4, L.2.6) Grade 3 (L.3.4, L.3.6) Grade 4 (L.4.4, L.4.6) Grade 5 (L.5.4, L.5.6) Grade 6 (L.6.4, L.6.6) Grade 7 (L.7.4, L.7.6) Grade 8 (L.8.4, L.8.6) Grades 9–10 (L.9–10.4, L.9–10.6) Grades 11–12 (L.11–12.4, L.11–12.6)
Frayer Model	Grades 3–5 (4.7) Grades 6–8 (4.3) Grades 9–12 (4.6)	Grade 3 (L.3.5, L.3.6) Grade 4 (L.4.5, L.4.6) Grade 5 (L.5.5, L.5.6) Grade 6 (L.6.5, L.6.6) Grade 7 (L.7.5, L.7.6) Grade 8 (L.8.5, L.8.6) Grades 9–10 (L.9–10.5, L.9–10.6) Grades 11–12 (L.11–12.5, L.11–12.6)
Vocabulary Self-Collection	Grades 1–2 (2.1) Grades 3–5 (2.1) Grades 6–8 (2.1) Grades 9–12 (2.1)	Grade 1 (L.1.4, L.1.6) Grade 2 (L.2.4, L.2.6) Grade 3 (L.3.4, L.3.6) Grade 4 (L.4.4, L.4.6) Grade 5 (L.5.4, L.5.6) Grade 6 (L.6.4, L.6.6) Grade 7 (L.7.4, L.7.6) Grade 8 (L.8.4, L.8.6) Grades 9–10 (L.9–10.4, L.9–10.6) Grades 11–12 (L.11–12.4, L.11–12.6)

Developing Vocabulary Overview (cont.)

Strategy	McREL Standards	Common Core State Standards
Possible Sentences	Grades 1–2 (1.2) Grades 3–5 (1.2) Grades 6–8 (1.2) Grades 9–12 (1.2)	Grade 1 (L.1.5, L.1.6) Grade 2 (L.2.5, L.2.6) Grade 3 (L.3.5, L.3.6) Grade 4 (L.4.5, L.4.6) Grade 5 (L.5.5, L.5.6) Grade 6 (L.6.5, L.6.6) Grade 7 (L.7.5, L.7.6) Grade 8 (L.8.5, L.8.6) Grades 9–10 (L.9–10.5, L.9–10.6) Grades 11–12 (L.11–12.5, L.11–12.6)
Word Trails	Grades 3–5 (4.3, 4.7) Grades 6–8 (4.3) Grades 9–12 (4.2)	Grade 3 (L.3.4, L.3.5) Grade 4 (L.4.4, L.4.5) Grade 5 (L.5.4, L.5.5) Grade 6 (L.6.4, L.6.5) Grade 7 (L.7.4, L.7.5) Grade 8 (L.8.4, L.8.5) Grades 9–10 (L.9–10.4, L.9–10.5) Grades 11–12 (L.11–12.4, L.11–12.5)
Word Questioning	Grades 3–5 (4.7) Grades 6–8 (4.3) Grades 9–12 (4.6)	Grade 3 (L.3.4, L.3.5) Grade 4 (L.4.4, L.4.5) Grade 5 (L.5.4, L.5.5) Grade 6 (L.6.4, L.6.5) Grade 7 (L.7.4, L.7.5) Grade 8 (L.8.4, L.8.5) Grades 9–10 (L.9–10.4, L.9–10.5) Grades 11–12 (L.11–12.4, L.11–12.5)
Open Word Sort	Grades 1–2 (4.2) Grades 3–5 (4.3, 4.7) Grades 6–8 (4.2, 4.3) Grades 9–12 (4.2, 4.6)	Grade 1 (L.1.4, L.1.5) Grade 2 (L.2.4, L.2.5) Grade 3 (L.3.4, L.3.5) Grade 4 (L.4.4, L.4.5) Grade 5 (L.5.4, L.5.5) Grade 6 (L.6.4, L.6.5) Grade 7 (L.7.4, L.7.5) Grade 8 (L.8.4, L.8.5) Grades 9–10 (L.9–10.4, L.9–10.5) Grades 11–12 (L.11–12.4, L.11–12.5)

Word Wall

Background Information

A Word Wall is a display of important grade-appropriate vocabulary or concept words. It can be created on a bulletin board or on a large sheet of paper taped to the wall. A Word Wall is an effective way to keep track of new grade-appropriate words students are learning. They also serve as an easy reference for students to use during class to develop oral and written language as they demonstrate their understanding of new vocabulary. Through their discussions, students determine and clarify the meanings of unknown words on the Word Wall and learn how to use these words in their speech and writing.

Grade Levels/Standards Addressed

See page 32 for the standards this strategy addresses, or refer to the Digital Resource CD (standards.pdf) to read the correlating standards in their entirety.

Stages of Writing Process

Prewrite, Draft, Revise

Activity

Prepare strips of cardstock that are large enough to be read easily from a distance, and ask students to neatly print the vocabulary words on them. Encourage students to include illustrations for each word, if possible. Designate a spot in the classroom for the Word Wall, and reserve a specific area for new vocabulary words. Remind students to use this resource as they write about, or learn, new concepts. A Word Wall can be used throughout the whole year with all of the vocabulary included in it, or you can create "mini Word Walls" specific to units of study. There are many activities that can be incorporated with the Word Wall. Select from the activities listed, or create activities to best meet the needs of your students to help them acquire and use accurately the new vocabulary:

- Make a List—Have students classify the Word Wall words by their part of speech, roots, affixes, etc.

- Defining Sentence—Assign each student a word. Students must create a sentence for the assigned word that gives the definition of the word.

- What's at the End?—Identify and discuss words with similar endings.

- See It, Say It, Chant It, Sing It, and Clap It!— Find as many different ways as possible to read and spell out loud the words on the Word Wall.

- Be a Mind Reader—Have a student give clues about a selected word while class members try to guess the word. Clues can include the beginning or ending letter; rhyme clues; the definition of its roots, prefixes, or suffixes; number of letters in the word, etc.

- Guess the Missing Word—Write sentences on the board using the Word Wall words and challenge students to guess which word belongs in each sentence.

Word Wall (cont.)

- Find It First!—Call two students up to the Word Wall at a time. Call out a word; see which student can find it first and use it in a sentence.

- Seek and Find—Challenge students to search newspapers, brochures, letters, business cards, etc., to highlight Word Wall words.

- Crossword Puzzles—Have students use the words on the Word Wall to make crossword puzzles, exchange crossword puzzles, and then solve them.

Differentiation

For English language learners, the Word Wall is particularly helpful because it exposes students to important vocabulary words and is an easy reference for students during the lesson. Give English language learners a list of the words to keep at their desks and take home for assignments, if necessary. Encourage above-level students to add more challenging words to the Word Wall. These students can generate a list of words they have an interest in learning. Give below-level students a copy of the words to place in their notebooks. They may need repeated explanations of the meanings and use of each word.

Grades 1–2 Example

Dinosaurs Before Dark by Mary Pope Osborne

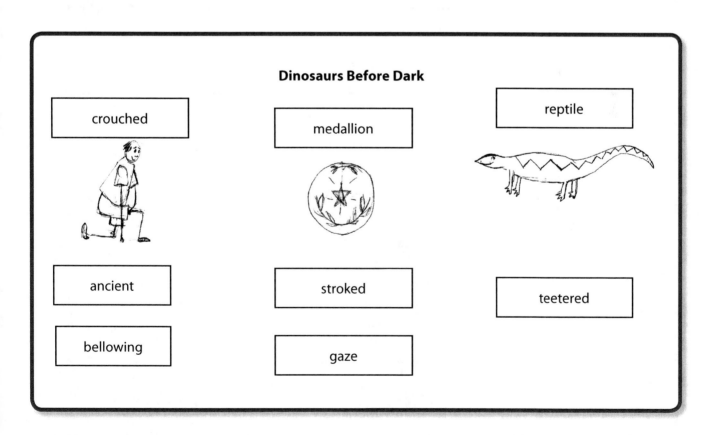

Dinosaurs Before Dark

crouched

medallion

reptile

ancient

stroked

teetered

bellowing

gaze

Word Wall (cont.)

Grades 3–5 Example

A Little Princess by Frances Hodgson Burnett

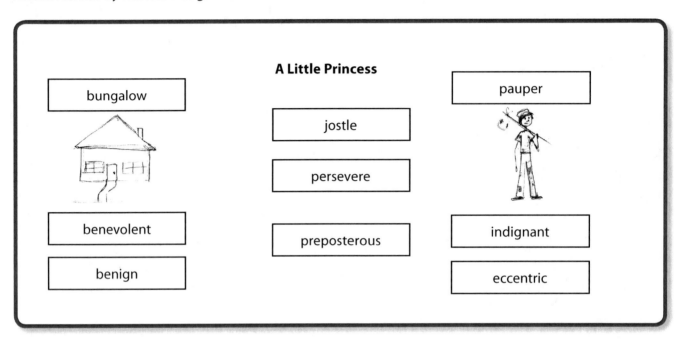

A Little Princess

bungalow

jostle

pauper

persevere

benevolent

indignant

benign

preposterous

eccentric

Grades 6–8 Example

The Alchemyst: The Secrets of the Immortal Nicholas Flamel by Michael Scott

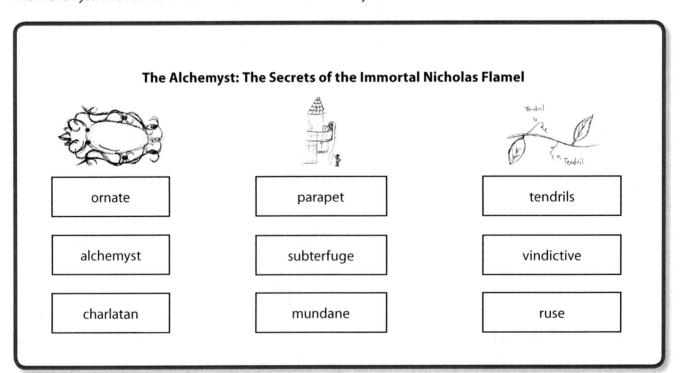

The Alchemyst: The Secrets of the Immortal Nicholas Flamel

ornate

parapet

tendrils

alchemyst

subterfuge

vindictive

charlatan

mundane

ruse

Word Wall *(cont.)*

Grades 9–12 Example

A Lesson Before Dying by Ernest J. Gaines

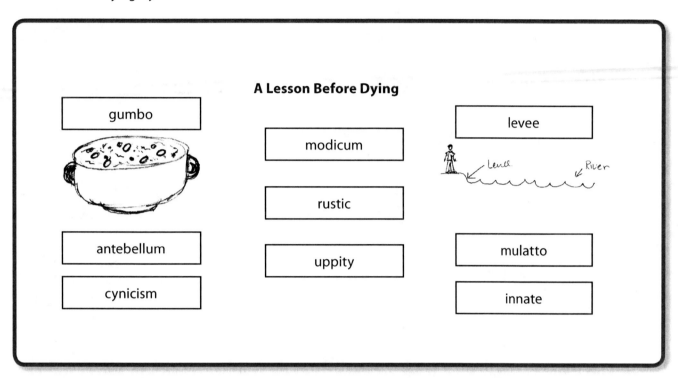

Frayer Model

Background Information

The Frayer Model (Frayer, Fredrick, and Klausmeier 1969), also known as a word map (Schwartz and Raphael 1985), is a strategy designed to help students understand relationships and similarities between concepts. This strategy uses a graphic organizer to help students understand a concept and recognize similarities and differences between that concept and other concepts being discussed. The framework of the Frayer Model consists of the concept word, the definition, characteristics of the concept word, examples of the concept word, and nonexamples of the concept word. A key element of this model is providing an example of what the concept is and what it is not. This strategy helps students understand the nuances of the concept and teaches them to derive meaning by comparing the words to their synonyms, antonyms, and other examples. The Frayer Model is often used when teaching vocabulary, but it can be used to teach and reinforce literary concepts as well.

Grade Levels/Standards Addressed

See page 32 for the standards this strategy addresses, or refer to the Digital Resource CD (standards.pdf) to read the correlating standards in their entirety.

Stage of Writing Process

Prewrite

Activity

Distribute the *Frayer Model* activity sheet (page 41, frayermodel.pdf). Have students write the concept of the lesson at the center. This may be a concept phrase or a single word, depending on the needs of students and the lesson objective. As a class, determine the definition of this concept. Students can use a variety of resources to develop a definition that is clear, concise, and easy to understand. Next, help students determine the characteristics or attributes of this concept. Finally, determine as a class what the concept is and what it is not. Encourage students to generate their own examples and nonexamples, and allow time for students to discuss their findings with the class. Once students are comfortable using this strategy, they can work in small groups, in pairs, or independently to research different concepts relating to fiction. When the graphic organizer has been completed, students then write a paragraph about this concept using the *Frayer Model* activity sheet as a guide.

Differentiation

Place English language learners in groups or pair them with partners to complete the activity. Working with a partner will help them learn how to complete the activity sheet, and they will also benefit greatly from the discussions. Call on above-level students to model how to complete the organizer for the class. Above-level students can work with two or three classmates to show the class how to complete the *Frayer Model*. The class can learn from watching this discussion, and it encourages above-level students to think through their reasoning. Provide one-on-one instruction during the small group work for below-level students, and select an appropriate concept word.

Frayer Model (cont.)

Grades 3–5 Example

Definition	Characteristics
the subject or topic of a text	can be straightforward or hidden in the text texts can have multiple themes the theme is often the moral of the story in fairy tales and fables the theme often explores big questions about humankind and other big ideas

Word

theme

Examples	Nonexamples
friendship, honesty, jealousy, betrayal, loyalty, courage, perseverance	plot, action, characters, tone

Grades 6–8 Example

Definition	Characteristics
the use of one object or action to represent something else	often used in literature to convey theme often appear periodically throughout the story the reader usually must infer the meaning of the symbols used in fiction

Word

symbolism

Examples	Nonexamples
snakes often symbolize evil or deception a winding road is used to represent a personal journey darkness often means death light symbolizes life and hope	a swimming pool is not a symbol for shelter a scary Halloween mask is not a symbol of kindness a book is not a symbol for ignorance

Frayer Model (cont.)

Grades 9–12 Example

Definition

an exaggeration purposely used to create emphasis or effect in literature

Characteristics

not meant to be taken literally

used to create strong feelings or dramatic impressions

often used in casual speech and poetry

type of figurative language

Word

hyperbole

Examples

He has a ton of money.

She is taller than a mountain.

I have a million things to do.

This bike goes faster than the speed of light.

Nonexamples

He has a lot of money.

She is as tall as my mother.

I have a lot of things to do.

This bike is really fast.

Frayer Model

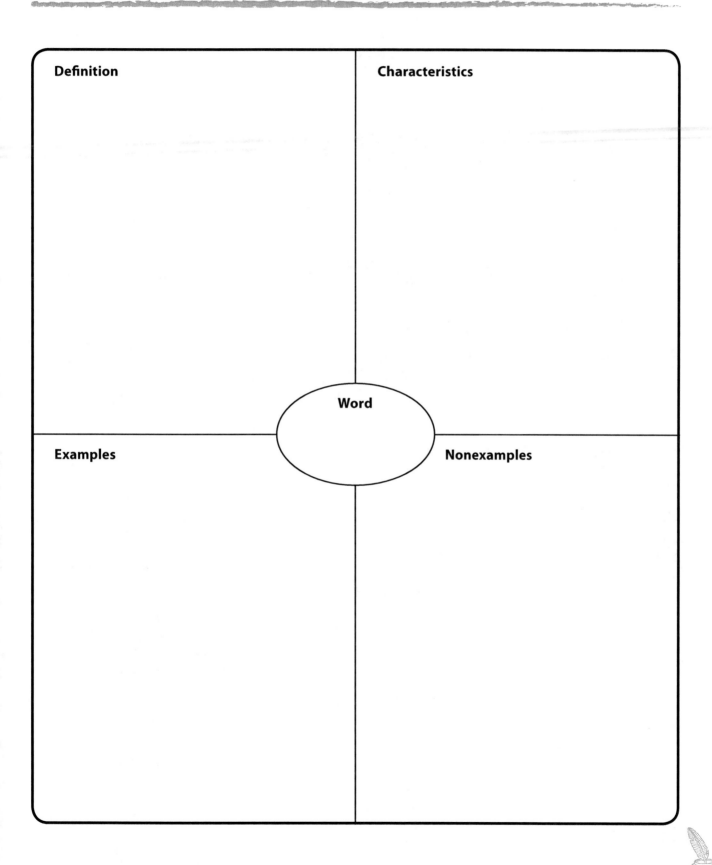

Definition

Characteristics

Word

Examples

Nonexamples

Vocabulary Self-Collection

Background Information

Martha Haggard (1982, 1986) designed the Vocabulary Self-Collection strategy to help students create a list of vocabulary words they would be interested in learning and researching. The strategy is meant to stimulate vocabulary growth and help students determine or clarify the meaning of unknown words. Research shows that the more exposure students have to the written word, the more their vocabulary increases. By generating lists of grade-appropriate words to study, students become more sensitive to and aware of words and their meanings.

Grade Levels/Standards Addressed

See page 32 for the standards this strategy addresses, or refer to the Digital Resource CD (standards.pdf) to read the correlating standards in their entirety.

Stage of Writing Process

Prewrite

Activity

Instruct students to create a list of words from their reading materials that they are interested in studying. The words can be either general academic vocabulary or domain-specific words, depending on the selected text. Have students review their lists and nominate words to be studied by the class. As you write these words on the board or display them with a document camera, ask students to define them and justify the selection of each word. Clarify the meaning of each word and clear up any misunderstandings, consulting the actual text or a dictionary if needed. Students may ask one another questions about the words and their definitions. After the discussion, challenge the class to decide which words should make the final cut. For example, delete words that most students already know, duplicates of words, and words of lesser interest to students. Have students write down the selected words and their meanings in their Vocabulary Journal (see pages 97–100) and post them on the Word Wall (see pages 34–37). Incorporate these words into lessons and writing activities that will reinforce definitions and understanding. Encourage students to use these words as often as possible in their own writing to move the new vocabulary words into their expressive languages.

Differentiation

During the discussion, clarify and elaborate further on some definitions, if necessary, to ensure that English language learners understand the meanings. Use visuals as well as thorough descriptions. Challenge above-level students to document the use of the vocabulary words in their personal writing assignments. Below-level students may need assistance articulating the meanings of difficult words, so encourage them to use visuals or drawings if needed.

Vocabulary Self-Collection *(cont.)*

Grades 1–2 Example

Text: It was crowded at the restaurant. A woman entered the room. She sat down to order. Her clothes were fancy and her hair was curly. I looked down at my jeans. They were torn. I quickly looked away from the woman, embarrassed of my clothes.

Nominated Words: crowded, order, fancy, curly, torn, embarrassed

Grades 3–5 Example

Text: I cautiously peered around the corner, hoping to spot the intruder. When I failed to see anyone, I hesitated and then slowly maneuvered my body closer to the doorway. My whole body felt tense as I prepared to flee if necessary.

Nominated Words: cautiously, intruder, hesitated, maneuvered, tense, flee

Grades 6–8 Example

Text: As she approached the dilapidated mansion, she began to smell a putrid odor. The smell seemed to be wafting through an open window on her right. Suddenly she stopped, bristling at a noise that came from inside the decrepit abode. She contemplated turning around, but she had come too far to abandon her mission at this point.

Nominated Words: dilapidated, putrid, odor, wafting, bristling, decrepit, abode, contemplated

Vocabulary Self-Collection *(cont.)*

Grades 9–12 Example

Text:

Lysander

Content with Hermia? No. I do repent
The tedious minutes I with her have spent.
Not Hermia but Helena I love.
Who will not change a raven for a dove?
The will of man is by his reason swayed,
And reason says you are the worthier maid.
Things growing are not ripe until their season,
So I, being young, till now ripe not to reason.
And touching now the point of human skill,
Reason becomes the marshal to my will
And leads me to your eyes, where I o'erlook
Love's stories written in love's richest book.

Helena

Wherefore was I to this keen mockery born?
When at your hands did I deserve this scorn?
Is 't not enough, is 't not enough, young man,
That I did never, no, nor never can,
Deserve a sweet look from Demetrius' eye,
But you must flout my insufficiency?
Good troth, you do me wrong; good sooth, you do,
In such disdainful manner me to woo.
But fare you well. Perforce I must confess
I thought you lord of more true gentleness.
Oh, that a lady of one man refused
Should of another be abused!

Nominated Words: repent, tedious, reason, marshal, wherefore, mockery, flout, insufficiency, troth, sooth, disdainful

from William Shakespeare's *A Midsummer Night's Dream*

Possible Sentences

Background Information

David Moore and Sharon Moore (1986) designed the Possible Sentences strategy as a way to teach vocabulary words introduced in a text. Other benefits of this strategy include making predictions about reading, providing a purpose for reading, and encouraging interest in text. Students learn to make predictions about new words, check their predictions, and use the text to rewrite and refine their predictions. This strategy not only helps students acquire and use new vocabulary words, but it also strengthens their abilities to develop their writing through revising and editing.

Grade Levels/Standards Addressed

See page 33 for the standards this strategy addresses, or refer to the Digital Resource CD (standards.pdf) to read the correlating standards in their entirety.

Stages of Writing Process

Draft, Revise

Activity

Make a list of important vocabulary words from the text and write them on the board or display them with a document camera. Read each word aloud to model correct pronunciation. Instruct students to select two words from the list to use in one sentence that might appear in a fictional narrative. Record sentences on the board, and underline each vocabulary word. Encourage students to generate sentences until all the vocabulary words have been used in at least one sentence. Remind students that good writers edit and revise their work, and have them read through the sentences again to make any needed changes.

Next, ask students to read the selected text and compare the class sentences with the actual sentences in the text. Students should take notes (or draw pictures for younger students) on meanings of words. After reading the text, carefully examine the sentences to see if they are written accurately. Have students explain how to edit and revise sentences, as needed. Call on students to write revised sentences independently using their new knowledge and understanding of these vocabulary words.

Differentiation

Preview the meanings of the vocabulary words with English language learners to ensure understanding. Encourage English language learners to draw pictures or write short phrases if they are not yet ready to write sentences. Ask above-level students to write multiple sentences using various forms of the words and more complicated sentence structures. Scaffold the strategy for below-level students by providing sentence frames. Also, encourage these students to extend their sentences by adding additional information.

Possible Sentences (cont.)

Grades 1–2 Example

Vocabulary Words:

fuss, squash, bush, helpless, kindness

Possible Sentences/Before Reading:

The kids <u>fussed</u>.
The ants <u>squashed</u> the food.
The bird was in the <u>bush</u>.
The <u>helpless</u> pony looked <u>kindness</u>.

Revised Sentences/After Reading:

A <u>fuss</u> began when the girl ate all the candy.
I <u>squashed</u> the ants.
The bird was trapped in the <u>bush</u>.
I looked at the <u>helpless</u> pony with kindness.

Grades 3–5 Example

Vocabulary Words:

animated, floundered, depressed, grasp, murky, wail

Possible Sentences/Before Reading:

One boy was <u>animated</u>, and the other seemed <u>depressed</u>.
The dog <u>floundered</u> about in the <u>murky</u> water.
She let out a <u>wail</u> when she lost her <u>grasp</u> on the railing.

Revised Sentences/After Reading:

When the boy saw the puppy, he lost his <u>depressed</u> expression and his face lit up in an <u>animated</u> smile.
When I dropped my ring in the dirty, <u>murky</u> water, I <u>floundered</u> about for more than half an hour trying to find it.
The baby stopped her high-pitched <u>wail</u> as soon as she had the bottle in her <u>grasp</u>.

Possible Sentences *(cont.)*

Grades 6–8 Example

Vocabulary Words:

brute, bellowed, anguish, undulating, soothing, dominated

Possible Sentences/Before Reading:

The <u>brute</u> <u>bellowed</u> loudly.
The <u>undulating</u> rhythm was <u>soothing</u>.
The large bear <u>dominated</u> the fight, causing the younger bear to cry out in <u>anguish</u>.

Revised Sentences/After Reading:

The victim <u>bellowed</u> loudly as the savage <u>brute</u> attacked him.
The <u>undulating</u> hills stretched as far as the eye could see and had a lulling, <u>soothing</u> effect on my anxiety.
After my competitor <u>dominated</u> me in the race, beating me by more than a minute, I was overcome with a feeling of deep <u>anguish</u> and distress.

Grades 9–12 Example

Vocabulary Words:

eccentric, spontaneous, persevere, contemplated, translucent, delirious

Possible Sentences/Before Reading:

After the man's <u>spontaneous</u> burst of song, people started calling him <u>eccentric</u>.
He <u>contemplated</u> the decision and decided to <u>persevere</u>.
The <u>translucent</u> liquid made him <u>delirious</u>.

Revised Sentences/After Reading:

His unconventional, <u>eccentric</u> views and <u>spontaneous</u> behavior made him unique and unforgettable.
He thought about his decision for quite a long time and <u>contemplated</u> all of the repercussions before deciding to <u>persevere</u> and continue with his mission.
His <u>translucent</u> skin seemed to glow, and his maniacal laughter made him appear <u>delirious</u>.

Word Trails

Background Information

A strong relationship exists between word knowledge and reading comprehension. Without word knowledge, students tend to read less and are more apt to be poor readers (Anderson and Freebody 1985). Seldom do words stand alone, isolated from, and unrelated, to other words. The Word Trails strategy helps students build connections, or "trails," from unknown words to familiar ones. These word relationships enable students to gain an understanding of unknown words through the examination of common grade-appropriate affixes and root words as well as the word's synonyms and antonyms. Students need to have a repertoire of strategies to use when they face unknown words in their reading, and the Word Trails strategy offers one such way to build meaning and word knowledge.

Grade Levels/Standards Addressed

See page 33 for the standards this strategy addresses, or refer to the Digital Resource CD (standards.pdf) to read the correlating standards in their entirety.

Stage of Writing Process

Prewrite

Activity

Introduce a new word and then build "trails" and connections from other words to it. The following are the main trails that connect words:

- root words—Many words in literature have similar root words. Knowing these can help students determine meaning.

- prefixes and suffixes—Recognizing and identifying prefixes or suffixes in a word can help determine its meaning.

- synonyms or similar words—Words become "friends" and can help students remember definitions. What are other words that have the same or similar meaning to the new word? What are examples of this word?

- antonyms—Identifying opposites is an effective way to clarify word meaning. What are the words that mean the opposite of this new word? What are nonexamples of the word?

Distribute the *Word Trails* activity sheet (page 50, wordtrails.pdf), and have students identify the trails from this word to other words. When finished, discuss students' findings. Primary grade teachers may want to complete the *Word Trails* activity sheet as a class and then post it on the Word Wall (pages 34–37). Students can add these words and their trails to their Vocabulary Journal (pages 97–100).

Differentiation

Preteach English language learners how to use the *Word Trails* activity sheet so they understand the format. Consider also preteaching the roots, prefixes, and suffixes that will be addressed during the whole-class lesson so that these students will be able to recognize them and apply meaning to the unknown vocabulary word. Use visuals whenever possible. Encourage above-level students to study additional or related vocabulary words and present and explain their Word Trails maps to the class. Limit the number of vocabulary words for below-level students to allow them to focus on a few words.

Word Trails *(cont.)*

Grades 3–5 Example

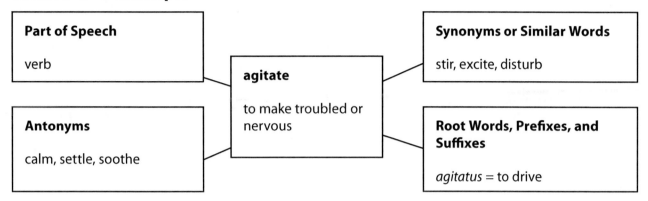

Part of Speech		Synonyms or Similar Words
verb	**agitate**	stir, excite, disturb
Antonyms	to make troubled or nervous	**Root Words, Prefixes, and Suffixes**
calm, settle, soothe		*agitatus* = to drive

Grades 6–8 Example

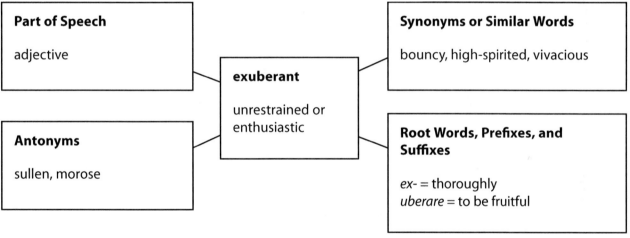

Part of Speech		Synonyms or Similar Words
adjective	**exuberant**	bouncy, high-spirited, vivacious
Antonyms	unrestrained or enthusiastic	**Root Words, Prefixes, and Suffixes**
sullen, morose		*ex-* = thoroughly *uberare* = to be fruitful

Grades 9–12 Example

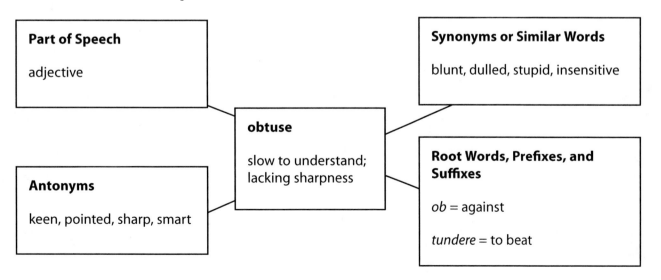

Part of Speech		Synonyms or Similar Words
adjective	**obtuse**	blunt, dulled, stupid, insensitive
Antonyms	slow to understand; lacking sharpness	**Root Words, Prefixes, and Suffixes**
keen, pointed, sharp, smart		*ob* = against *tundere* = to beat

Word Trails

Directions: Write the word that you are studying in the center box. Use resources to determine the root words, prefixes and suffixes, synonyms or similar words, and antonyms, and write them in the Word Trails graphic organizer.

Part of Speech	**Synonyms or Similar Words**

Antonyms	**Root Words, Prefixes, and Suffixes**

Word Questioning

Background Information

The Word Questioning strategy (Allen 1999, as cited in Bintz 2011) teaches students to examine words from a variety of angles using a series of questions built around Bloom's Taxonomy. These questions are designed to utilize a variety of skills, ranging from identifying basic knowledge about the word's definition to the more complex skills of analyzing and evaluating. This strategy is particularly useful for important concepts or domain-specific topics that require greater understanding in order to facilitate learning. By studying the word from a variety of perspectives, students gain an in-depth understanding of the word's meaning and develop personal connections with the word, allowing for better comprehension and recall. Through this strategy, students learn about the subtle nuances of the word's meaning and how the new word relates to other words. This type of thorough understanding enables students to utilize new vocabulary words with confidence in both their verbal and written work.

Grade Levels/Standards Addressed

See page 33 for the standards this strategy addresses, or refer to the Digital Resource CD (standards.pdf) to read the correlating standards in their entirety.

Stage of Writing Process

Prewrite

Activity

Introduce the class to the categories of Bloom's Taxonomy (Remembering, Understanding, Applying, Analyzing, Evaluating, and Creating), and explain how these categories are arranged so that each new level provides a deeper type of word knowledge. Tell students that they can use questions from each level of Bloom's Taxonomy to gain greater knowledge about new or unknown words. Display the *Word Questioning* activity sheet (page 55, wordquestioning.pdf) on the board or with a document camera, and select a word to use as an example. Write the novel word in the center rectangle and then ask students to help you fill in the other boxes by answering the designated questions. Once students are comfortable with the strategy, distribute the *Word Questioning* activity sheet to students and ask them to complete the activity sheet using a specific word. The chosen word should represent an important concept in the unit, reading, or activity. If there are multiple relevant topics, you may decide to let students choose a word from a short list.

Provide students with dictionaries and other reference books so they can research the word. Upon completion, ask all students to share their work with a partner. Then, hold a class discussion to summarize the new learning. Add the new word to your classroom's Word Wall (see pages 34–37), and encourage students to use it in their speech and writing.

Differentiation

Preview the questions with English language learners before commencing the activity, and allow these students to work with a partner for the duration of the activity. Below-level students will benefit from leveled reference materials that will allow them to research and comprehend the word's meaning. Above-level students should be encouraged to expound on the higher-level categories in the diagram (Analysis, Synthesis, and Evaluation).

Word Questioning (cont.)

Grades 3–5 Example

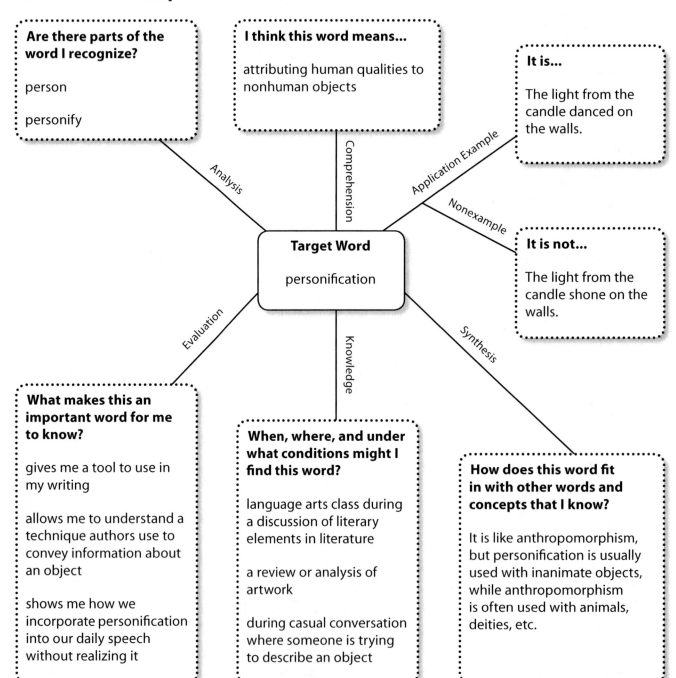

Are there parts of the word I recognize?

person

personify

I think this word means...

attributing human qualities to nonhuman objects

It is...

The light from the candle danced on the walls.

Analysis

Comprehension

Application Example

Nonexample

Target Word

personification

It is not...

The light from the candle shone on the walls.

Evaluation

Knowledge

Synthesis

What makes this an important word for me to know?

gives me a tool to use in my writing

allows me to understand a technique authors use to convey information about an object

shows me how we incorporate personification into our daily speech without realizing it

When, where, and under what conditions might I find this word?

language arts class during a discussion of literary elements in literature

a review or analysis of artwork

during casual conversation where someone is trying to describe an object

How does this word fit in with other words and concepts that I know?

It is like anthropomorphism, but personification is usually used with inanimate objects, while anthropomorphism is often used with animals, deities, etc.

Word Questioning *(cont.)*

Grades 6–8 Example

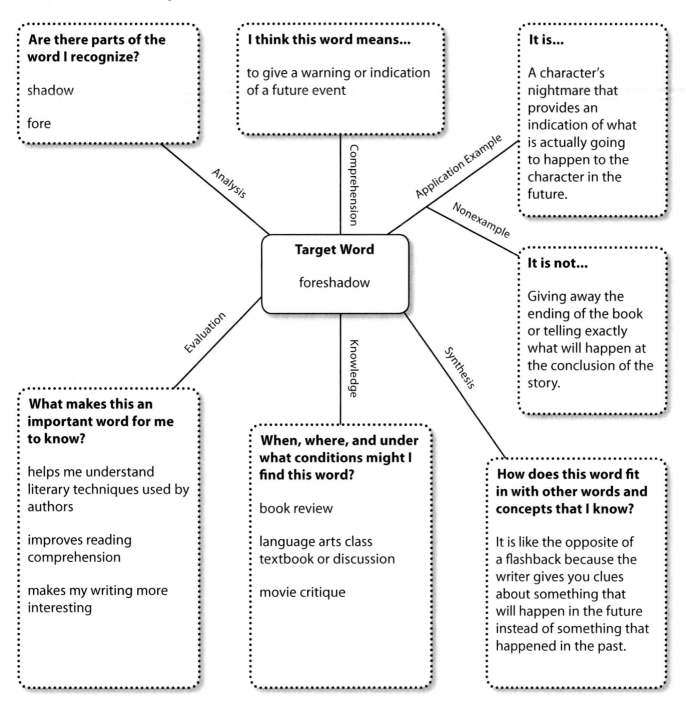

Are there parts of the word I recognize?

shadow

fore

I think this word means...

to give a warning or indication of a future event

It is...

A character's nightmare that provides an indication of what is actually going to happen to the character in the future.

Analysis

Comprehension

Application Example

Nonexample

Target Word

foreshadow

Evaluation

Knowledge

Synthesis

It is not...

Giving away the ending of the book or telling exactly what will happen at the conclusion of the story.

What makes this an important word for me to know?

helps me understand literary techniques used by authors

improves reading comprehension

makes my writing more interesting

When, where, and under what conditions might I find this word?

book review

language arts class textbook or discussion

movie critique

How does this word fit in with other words and concepts that I know?

It is like the opposite of a flashback because the writer gives you clues about something that will happen in the future instead of something that happened in the past.

Word Questioning *(cont.)*

Grades 9–12 Example

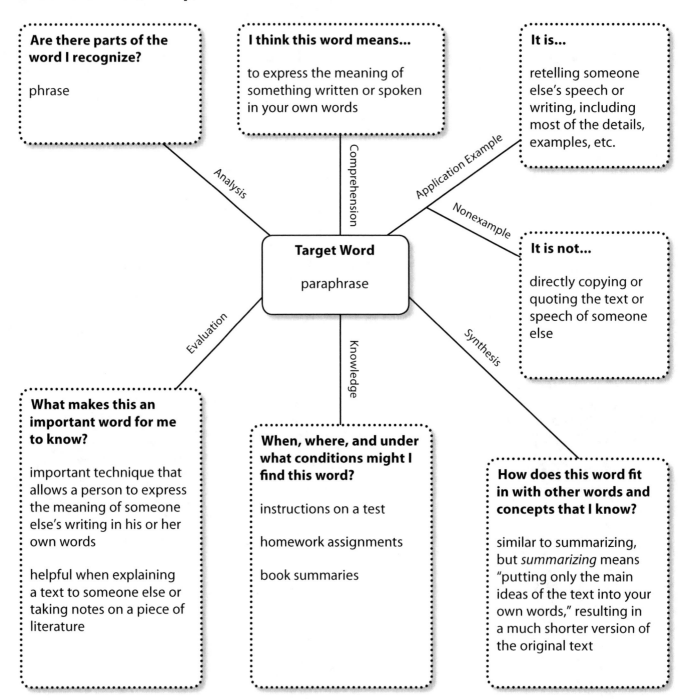

Are there parts of the word I recognize?

phrase

I think this word means...

to express the meaning of something written or spoken in your own words

It is...

retelling someone else's speech or writing, including most of the details, examples, etc.

Analysis

Comprehension

Application Example

Nonexample

Target Word

paraphrase

It is not...

directly copying or quoting the text or speech of someone else

Evaluation

Knowledge

Synthesis

What makes this an important word for me to know?

important technique that allows a person to express the meaning of someone else's writing in his or her own words

helpful when explaining a text to someone else or taking notes on a piece of literature

When, where, and under what conditions might I find this word?

instructions on a test

homework assignments

book summaries

How does this word fit in with other words and concepts that I know?

similar to summarizing, but *summarizing* means "putting only the main ideas of the text into your own words," resulting in a much shorter version of the original text

Word Questioning

Directions: Use the question prompts in each box to fill out more information about the new or unknown word. Consult a dictionary or other reference book when necessary.

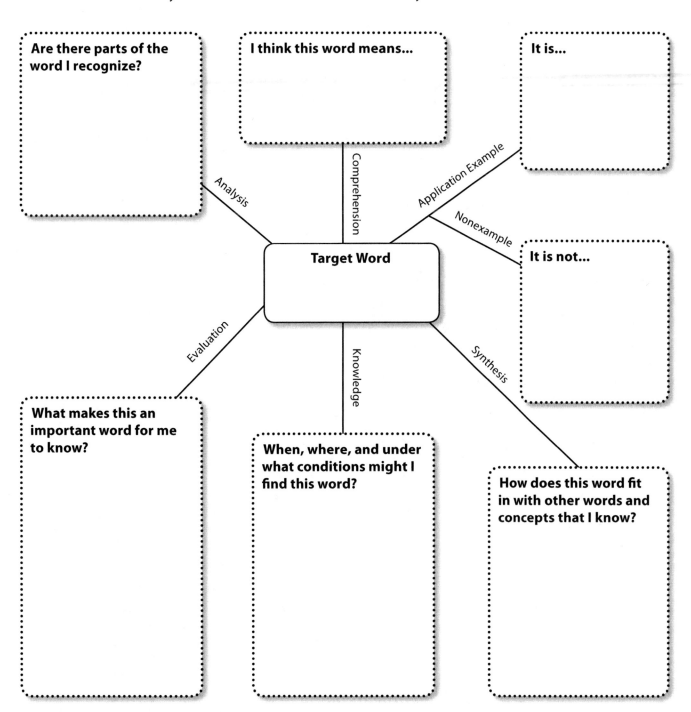

Adapted from Allen 1999 (cited in Bintz 2011)

Open Word Sort

Background Information

Through the Open Word Sort strategy, students learn to organize and remember new vocabulary words by sorting them into categories of their own creation. This activity not only elicits background knowledge, but it also enables students to make personalized connections between the words that will enhance their comprehension and recall of new words (Johns and Berglund 2010). By developing their own categories, students are tasked with forming tentative rules that govern the placement of words. In order to create these rules, students must examine the words from multiple perspectives and identify similarities and differences between words across a wide range of attributes. As students commence sorting the words into categories, they must further redefine the dimensions of each category as they encounter new words, adding and removing words as necessary. At the end of the activity, students explain their sorting rules in a written summary.

Grade Levels/Standards Addressed

See page 33 for the standards this strategy addresses, or refer to the Digital Resource CD (standards.pdf) to read the correlating standards in their entirety.

Stage of Writing Process

Prewrite

Activity

Select a variety of new or unknown words from an upcoming unit, reading selection, or project. Ideally, most students will have some general knowledge of the words but will not already know the precise definitions. For younger students who have never done an Open Word Sort, start by reviewing the concept of sorting using objects (e.g., colored tiles of various sizes) or well-known words. Make sure to highlight how the same group of objects or words can be sorted in multiple different ways, depending on the rules used to govern the sort. After you have established the concept of sorting, review the list of words with the class. Hold a class discussion to allow students to determine or clarify the words' meanings. Have students use dictionaries or other reference materials to look up precise definitions for words that are unfamiliar to most students. Next, discuss different parameters that students can use to sort the words. Here are some common possibilities:

- definition: students sort words into groups based on their meaning (e.g., *field*, *prairie*, *grassland*)

- etymology: students create categories based on shared affixes or root words (e.g., *examine*, *exterminate*, *experiment*)

- spelling patterns: students sort words into categories based on similar spelling patterns (e.g., words that contain *-ight* such as *fright*, *bright*, *tight*, *almighty*)

Distribute a list of the new words to students, and have them write each word on an index card. Alternatively, photocopy the words onto cardstock and have students cut them apart to create individual cards. Give students time to create their categories and sort their words. Emphasize that each category does not need to have the same number of words in it. After students are done sorting, have them record their word sort on the *Open Word Sort* activity sheet (page 60, wordsort. pdf). Next, ask students to write about their

Open Word Sort *(cont.)*

experience sorting the words and the rules they created to sort them. This can be done on students' activity sheets or in their Vocabulary Journals (see pages 97–100). To conclude the lesson, bring students back together and ask them to explain how they chose to sort their words and what they have learned from the activity.

Differentiation

This activity may be particularly challenging for English language learners because of the large number of unknown words introduced through the activity. Prior to the activity, provide English language learners with a list of the new words and their definitions to study the night before the activity. Both English language learners and below-level students will benefit from sorting a reduced number of words. Above-level students should be challenged to develop multiple ways to sort the words and explain their sorting rules clearly in their writing.

Open Word Sort *(cont.)*

Grades 1–2 Example

deed	early
nibble	might
worry	show
free	train
greedy	

Description: I decided to sort my words into two groups. The first group has words that have double letters and the second group has words that do not have double letters. I chose to use this sorting rule because I like how it is easy to notice double letters just by looking at the word. I think it makes those words stick out, and it helps me remember them.

Grades 3–5 Example

revert	capable	saunter
retire	desirable	reign
retain	sociable	gorge
resemble	unbearable	astound
		bungle

Description: I sorted my words according to their prefixes and suffixes. The first category contains words with the prefix *re-*. I looked up the prefix *re-* in the dictionary, and it means "again," so I learned that all the words in the first column are about doing something again. The second category contains words that share the suffix *-able*. I confirmed in the dictionary that this suffix means "able to." The third category contains words that do not share a common prefix or suffix with the other words. I found it helpful to sort my words this way because it is easier to remember what they mean when you understand the meaning of a word's prefix or suffix.

Open Word Sort (cont.)

Grades 6–8 Example

idyllic	timid	gingerly	caustic
serene	domineering	efficiently	respectful
pastoral	reclusive		estranged

Description: I noticed that all of the words on the list are either adjectives or adverbs, so I decided to sort my words according to whom or what they describe. The first column has words that describe a location or setting. In this case, all three words relate to a peaceful and calm setting. The second category includes adjectives used to describe people or characters. The third column is dedicated to adverbs that describe actions. The fourth and final category contains words that can describe relationships between two or more people. I found this sorting activity to be helpful because it made me notice the part of speech for each of the words and how these words relate to one another. Even though all of these words have different definitions, they all share the common purpose of describing something.

Grades 9–12 Example

deceitful	tumultuous	minuscule	jurisdiction	desolate
fraudulent	turbulent	microscopic	governance	barren
delusive	boisterous	infinitesimal		impoverished
		miniature		stark

Description: I conducted my sort based on the definitions of the words. The words in the first column all relate to dishonest qualities or behavior. The second category of words describes sudden, violent, or destructive characteristics. The words in the third column pertain to the very small size of something. The fourth category contains only two words, and these words describe political control over an area. The words in the last column relate to the quality of being empty or lacking. I chose to sort the words in this manner because I can remember them and their definitions more easily when I relate them to other similar words. I also find it helpful to know multiple synonyms for various words because it makes my writing more interesting and accurate if I have more words to choose from when I want to describe something.

Name: _____ **Date:** _____

Open Word Sort

Directions: Study the vocabulary words and determine ways in which they relate to one another. Sort the words into categories, and record your sort on the chart. When finished sorting, describe how you sorted the words. Be sure to include the rules you used to sort, why you chose to use these rules, and how this activity helped you understand the new words.

Description: _____

_____

_____

_____

Previewing and Reviewing Overview

Activating Prior Knowledge

Prior knowledge can be defined as any information that we know on a given topic before we begin learning new information. Research shows that activating background knowledge increases students' comprehension of new material (Christen and Murphy 1991). Accessing students' prior knowledge opens the doors for the new knowledge to find a place. Teachers who link new information to students' background knowledge encourage curiosity and provide a purpose for the new information. This enables the teacher to build on this knowledge while also motivating students to read. Through the activation of prior knowledge, students are able to make personal connections and incorporate these new thoughts and ideas into what they read and write about.

Reviewing and Spiral Knowledge

We all use scripts and categorical rules to interpret the world. When new information arises, our brains work to see how it fits with our predetermined ideas and scripts (Widmayer et al. 2004). Throughout our lives we constantly add to our knowledge base; this concept is known as *spiral knowledge* (Poplin 1988, as cited by Dechant 1991).

Using Expressive Writing

Expressive writing leads to the discovery and reinforcement of concepts being taught, so it is appropriate for previewing and reviewing activities. Toby Fulwiler (1980, 16) states, "Every time students write, they individualize instruction; the act of silent writing, even for five minutes, generates ideas, observations, emotions…regular writing makes it harder for students to remain passive." Through expressive writing, students are able to gather information, put the concepts into their own words, and begin to own it. Writing is another way for the brain to make sense of information and learning (Emig 1977).

When students use writing as a strategy to help them make sense of what they are reading and learning, they are writing to learn. This is often called *expressive writing*. It is a vital piece of the language arts curriculum because it allows students the opportunity to express their ideas about, and respond to, what they are learning.

There is a variety of expressive writing activities: journals, KWL (Ogle 1986), T-List, free writes, dialogue journals (Atwell 1984; Harste, Short, and Burke 1988), problem analyses, learning logs, peer dialogues, and many more. Many of these strategies will be explained and described in this section of the book. With expressive writing, students are encouraged to use their own vocabulary, and the emphasis is on the content and understanding of the student, not on the writing mechanics. Sharon Hamilton-Weiler (1988) explains that this kind of writing is ". . . a way into, or means of learning, a way into understanding through articulating."

Previewing and Reviewing Overview (cont.)

Standards Addressed

The following chart shows the correlating standards for each strategy in this section. Refer to the Digital Resource CD (standards.pdf) to read the correlating standards in their entirety.

Strategy	McREL Standards	Common Core State Standards
Think Sheet	Grades 1–2 (1.1, 1.2) Grades 3–5 (1.1, 1.2) Grades 6–8 (1.1, 1.2) Grades 9–12 (1.1, 1.2)	Grade 1 (W.1.5, W.1.8) Grade 2 (W.2.5, W.2.8) Grade 3 (W.3.5, W.3.8) Grade 4 (W.4.5, W.4.8) Grade 5 (W.5.5, W.5.8) Grade 6 (W.6.5, W.6.8) Grade 7 (W.7.5, W.7.8) Grade 8 (W.8.5, W.8.8) Grades 9–10 (W.9–10.5, W.9–10.8) Grades 11–12 (W.11–12.5, W.11–12.8)
Free-Association Brainstorming	Grades 1–2 (1.1) Grades 3–5 (1.1) Grades 6–8 (1.1) Grades 9–12 (1.1)	Grade 1 (W.1.8) Grade 2 (W.2.8) Grade 3 (W.3.8) Grade 4 (W.4.8) Grade 5 (W.5.8) Grade 6 (W.6.8) Grade 7 (W.7.8) Grade 8 (W.8.8) Grades 9–10 (W.9–10.8) Grades 11–12 (W.11–12.8)
Guided Free Write	Grades 1–2 (1.8) Grades 3–5 (1.5, 1.6, 1.10) Grades 6–8 (1.5) Grades 9–12 (1.5, 1.6)	Grade 1 (CCRA.W.10) Grade 2 (CCRA.W.10) Grade 3 (W.3.10) Grade 4 (W.4.10) Grade 5 (W.5.10) Grade 6 (W.6.10) Grade 7 (W.7.10) Grade 8 (W.8.10) Grades 9–10 (W.9–10.10) Grades 11–12 (W.11–12.10)

Previewing and Reviewing Overview *(cont.)*

Strategy	McREL Standards	Common Core State Standards
End-of-Class Reflection	Grades 1–2 (1.6) Grades 3–5 (1.11) Grades 6–8 (1.12) Grades 9–12 (1.12)	Grade 1 (CCRA.W.10, W.1.8) Grade 2 (CCRA.W.10, W.2.8) Grade 3 (W.3.8, W.3.10) Grade 4 (W.4.8, W.4.10) Grade 5 (W.5.8, W.5.10) Grade 6 (W.6.8, W.6.10) Grade 7 (W.7.8, W.7.10) Grade 8 (WW.8.8, .8.10) Grades 9–10 (W.9–10.8, W.9–10.10) Grades 11–12 (W.11–12.8, W.11–12.10)
Reader-Response Writing Chart	Grades 3–5 (1.4, 1.10, 1.11) Grades 6–8 (1.4, 1.12) Grades 9–12 (1.4, 1.12)	Grade 3 (CCRA.W.9, W.3.10) Grade 4 (W.4.9, .4.10) Grade 5 (W.5.9, W.5.10) Grade 6 (W.6.9, W.6.10) Grade 7 (W.7.9, W.7.10) Grade 8 (W.8.9, W.8.10) Grades 9–10 (W.9–10.9, W.9–10.10) Grades 11–12 (W.11–12.9, W.11–12.10)
Story Impressions	Grades 1–2 (1.1, 1.2) Grades 3–5 (1.1, 1.2) Grades 6–8 (1.1, 1.2) Grades 9–12 (1.1, 1.2)	Grade 1 (CCRA.W.9, W.1.8) Grade 2 (CCRA.W.9, W.2.8) Grade 3 (CCRA.W.9, W.3.8) Grade 4 (W.4.8, W.4.9) Grade 5 (W.5.8, W.5.9) Grade 6 (W.6.8, W.6.9) Grade 7 (W.7.8, W.7.9) Grade 8 (W.8.8, W.8.9) Grades 9–10 (W.9–10.8, W.9–10.9) Grades 11–12 (W.11–12.8, W.11–12.9)
Story Prediction Chart	Grades 1–2 (1.1, 1.2) Grades 3–5 (1.1, 1.2)	Grade 1 (CCRA.W.9, W.1.8) Grade 2 (CCRA.W.9, W.2.8) Grade 3 (CCRA.W.9, W.3.8) Grade 4 (W.4.8, W.4.9) Grade 5 (W.5.8, W.5.9)

Think Sheet

Background Information

The Think Sheet strategy enables students to examine their knowledge about a certain topic before reading about it and then compare that to what they learn after reading or discussion. This strategy provides practice in recalling relevant information related to a topic, a skill that students need to learn for the prewriting phase. Students also gain practice in developing and strengthening their writing when they revise their notes to reflect their new knowledge after reading the selected text. Both skills are keys to successful writing.

Grade Levels/Standards Addressed

See page 62 for the standards this strategy addresses, or refer to the Digital Resource CD (standards.pdf) to read the correlating standards in their entirety.

Stages of Writing Process

Prewrite, Revise

Preparation

Prior to a reading or a discussion, formulate some questions about the topic that will activate prior knowledge, generate thinking, and promote curiosity. Then add the questions to the *Think Sheet* activity sheet (page 68, thinksheet.pdf).

Activity

Distribute the prepared *Think Sheet* activity sheet, display it using a document camera, or re-create it on the board or on chart paper. Present the main issue to the class, and ask students to answer the questions and write down what they know. Encourage them to write any questions that they have about the topic because questions stimulate more learning. Collect students' activity sheets and then assign the reading or complete the activity as planned. Redistribute the *Think Sheet* activity sheets so that students can use their new knowledge to edit their original answers. Ask questions such as "How did your knowledge change after this activity? Can you add any additional information? Do you have any questions that were not answered? Were any of your original thoughts inaccurate?" Encourage students to write additional questions they have on the topic. Allow them to share what they have learned from the reading, and encourage them to make connections among their questions, their thoughts, and the information presented in the text.

Variation

Complete this activity as a class with primary grade students. Lead a brief discussion about each question, and ask students to help develop an answer. You may choose specific students to help write some or all of the sentences on the board.

Differentiation

Clarify the questions asked of English language learners by discussing unknown words or new concepts. Remind students that these are new questions and they are not expected to know the answers. Encourage above-level students to conduct further research to answer the questions left unanswered. Scaffold the activity with some completed responses for below-level students. If the reading level is too high, read aloud to them or have them do a paired reading.

Think Sheet *(cont.)*

Grades 1–2 Example (before reading)

Title: *The Perfect Pony* by Kimberly Brubaker Bradley

Teacher Questions	My Questions/Thoughts
1. What type of things do you need to do to take care of a horse? You need to give it water, feed it, and clean its stall. 2. What kinds of traits can a horse have? Horses can be gentle, wild, fast, slow, old, or young. 3. How do you feel when you have to wait a long time to get something you really want? I feel like time is slow when I am excited about something. I can be impatient.	I know that horses need a lot of care when you have one as a pet. Some horses are nice to ride, and some are more difficult. Can all horses be trained to be ridden? How old do you have to be to have your own horse?

Grades 3–5 Example (after reading)

Title: *Pippi Longstocking* by Astrid Lindgren

Teacher Questions	My Questions/Thoughts
1. What would you do all day if you lived in a house without any grownups? I would sleep in late, eat lots of ice cream, play with my friends. 2. Do you think you would enjoy not having any rules in your house? Yes, it would be fun to do whatever I wanted. 3. How do children use their imaginations to entertain themselves? They create imaginary worlds and stories.	Pippi definitely has a different lifestyle because she lives by herself without any grownups. I don't think that I would be very happy living like she does. People think that she is very strange, but she doesn't care. Is it really possible for a girl to live by herself without any grownups?

Think Sheet (cont.)

Grades 6–8 Example (after reading)

Title: *A Day No Pigs Would Die* by Robert Newton Peck

Teacher Questions	My Questions/Thoughts
1. What is the relationship between a farmer and his or her animals? I think some farmers view their animals only as a source of money and some have more complex relationships with them. 2. What is a Shaker? I think a Shaker is someone who belongs to the Shaker religion. 3. How does labeling people affect other people's expectations? Labels can help you understand someone better, but they can also be hurtful. Labels cause you to expect certain things from a person, but often, these assumptions are not accurate because every person is different.	How does Robert Peck feel about being a Shaker? Why does Robert kiss his father's hand after they butcher Pinky? Will Robert choose to maintain his father's farm and continue to slaughter pigs?

Think Sheet (cont.)

Grades 9–12 Example (after reading)

Title: *A Death in the Family* by James Agee

Teacher Questions	My Questions/Thoughts
1. How can religion affect people's relationships with one another? If people share the same religion, it can bring them together. If people have different religions, or one is religious and one is not, it can cause tension in the relationship. 2. How do children deal with death differently from how adults do? Children deal with death in different ways, but often, their naiveté about the world makes them more accepting and less fearful of death. 3. How do authors use characters' memories to develop their stories? By discussing characters' memories or flashbacks, authors provide the reader with information about past events that have helped shape the characters' personalities and lives.	Why does the author choose to tell the story from Rufus's perspective? Why did the author choose Tennessee for the setting of the book? The ending of this book is very ambiguous. The author does not clarify how Rufus feels about religion and the beliefs of his mother and aunt. I think the author did this on purpose to make the story more realistic.

Think Sheet

Directions: Write your answers to the questions from your teacher. After the reading assignment or activity, write any thoughts or questions that you have about the topic.

Title: _____

Teacher Questions	My Questions/Thoughts

Free-Association Brainstorming

Background Information

The Free-Association Brainstorming strategy encourages divergent thinking for students and helps them generate many ideas on a given subject. It also helps students access their prior knowledge on the subject being studied without requiring them to organize that information. Often, students have some content knowledge but are not prepared to organize it in a systematic fashion. This strategy is the beginning of the writing process.

Grade Levels/Standards Addressed

See page 62 for the standards this strategy addresses, or refer to the Digital Resource CD (standards.pdf) to read the correlating standards in their entirety.

Stage of Writing Process

Prewrite

Activity

Distribute the *Free-Association Brainstorming* activity sheet (page 72, freeassociation.pdf) to students to help them in planning their written work during the prewriting phase. Write the topic on the board, and have students write it at the center of the map. Do not discuss this topic or explain it. Instruct students to write in the surrounding circles any words, thoughts, ideas, or examples that come to mind. If there are too few circles, students can continue to add more. Next, meet as a class and share all the ideas that students came up with. Remind them that they may continue to think of new ideas and can add them to their maps. The maps can be used as a springboard to writing or as a way to access and/or organize prior knowledge on the subject being studied.

Variation

In primary grade classes, this activity is best completed as a class because it is meant to focus on the prewriting process of generating ideas—both good and bad—as quickly as possible. Write students' contributions on the board so that writing will not hinder them. Use of the *Free-Association Brainstorming* activity sheet can be altered to fit the needs of the lesson and students: It can be used independently (to assess each student's prior knowledge), in pairs or small groups (to generate additional ideas), or as a whole class (to allow for teacher prompting, modeling, or scaffolding).

Differentiation

Encourage English language learners to draw pictures or diagrams if that helps them communicate their ideas more easily. Challenge above-level students with a more complex concept that requires higher-order thinking skills. Have below-level students work with partners to assist in getting their ideas on paper. Remind them that the purpose is simply to get their ideas on paper without worrying about spelling or grammar.

Free-Association Brainstorming (cont.)

Grades 1–2 Example

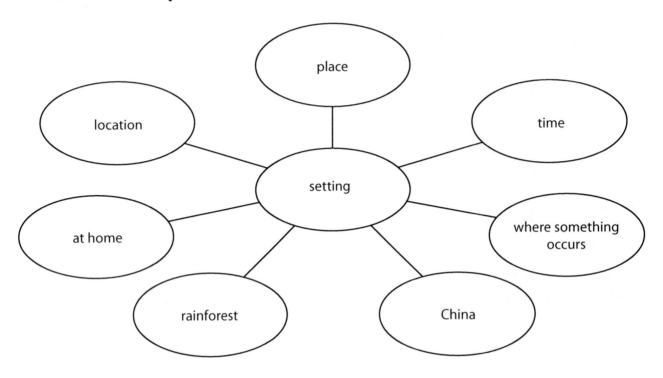

Grades 3–5 Example

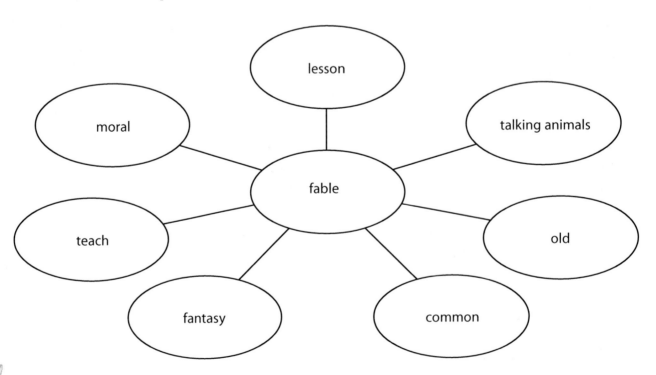

Free-Association Brainstorming *(cont.)*

Grades 6–8 Example

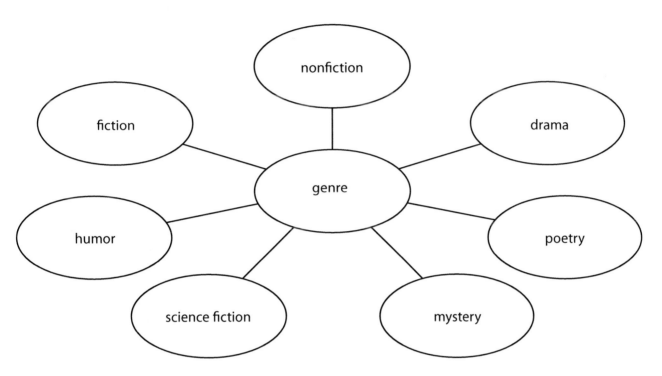

Grades 9–12 Example

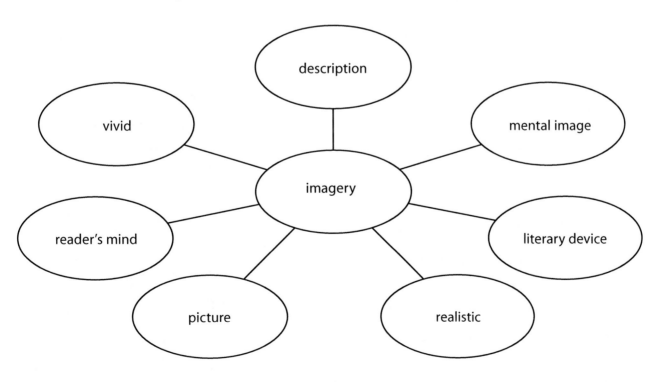

Free-Association Brainstorming

Directions: Write the topic in the center oval. Then, add any words, thoughts, ideas, or examples in the surrounding ovals.

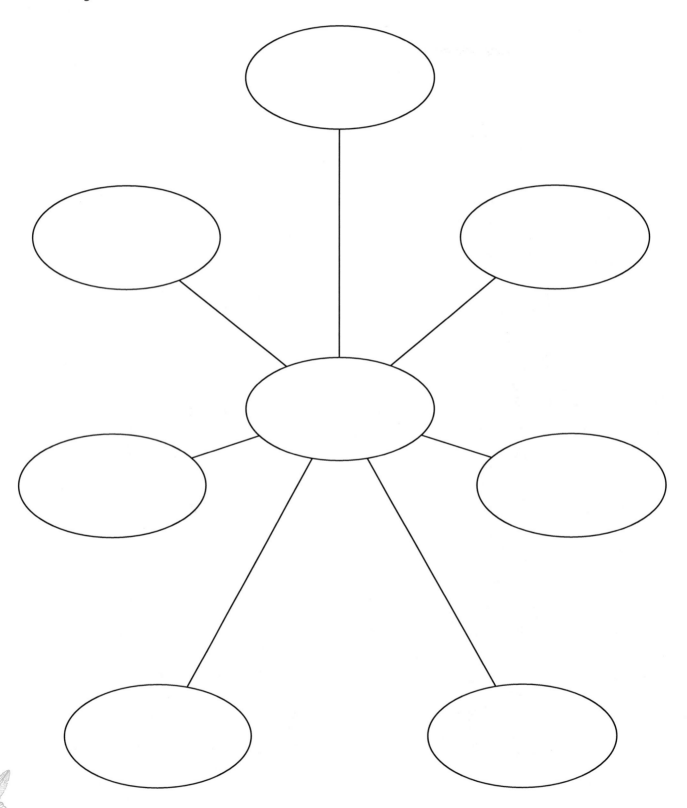

Guided Free Write

Background Information

The Guided Free Write strategy, introduced by Peter Elbow (1973), is a form of free writing. The difference is that students are guided in the topics they write about instead of writing about whatever comes to mind. Using this strategy in a language arts class encourages students to write for a designated amount of time about their thoughts and experiences related to classroom topics and discussions. It encourages students to record observations about what they are learning and to generate questions about literature. The Guided Free Write strategy allows students to practice writing using literary terms and concepts with support from the teacher. This practice builds confidence in writing, enhances vocabulary development, cements understanding, and leads to further discovery. This "thinking through" helps them clarify exactly what it is they do not understand. The primary focus is not on spelling, grammar, or mechanics. The intent is for students to think and write about their thinking.

Grade Levels/Standards Addressed

See page 62 for the standards this strategy addresses, or refer to the Digital Resource CD (standards.pdf) to read the correlating standards in their entirety.

Stage of Writing Process

Draft

Activity

Prepare for the Guided Free Write by thinking of the central concept or theme pertaining to the fictional literature that is being taught, and determine a question or questions that will generate thought about the subject. Asking questions as opposed to describing a concept encourages higher-order thinking. These questions can be controversial or may simply encourage students to think further on a given topic. To begin, write the question on the board and instruct students to write on this topic in a notebook or on a sheet of paper. Here are some suggestions for using Guided Free Writes:

- Be sure all students have access to paper and pencils so they can spend the entire time thinking and writing.

- Tell students not to cross out any information but rather to continually add to their writing. There are no bad ideas. Many of these beginning thoughts will lead to new ideas or trails of thought.

- Keep the classroom free of distractions and noise so that students can focus on their writing.

- Set a timer for 10–20 minutes. This may differ depending on students' ages and the purpose of the Guided Free Write. Remind students that if they are actively thinking on the topic, then it is okay to pause in their writing.

- Remind students not to focus on spelling, grammar, or punctuation. The focus is about getting ideas on paper.

Guided Free Write (cont.)

Variation

Allow students in the primary grades to draw pictures along with writing or typing to explain their thoughts. You may choose to have some students complete the Guided Free Write on the computer. Both typing on the computer and writing on paper provide students with informal writing experience.

Differentiation

Allow English language learners to write words or phrases or draw pictures related to what they are thinking about. Provide sentence frames to model how to begin the answers. Encourage English language learners to put concepts down on paper and not to worry about correct tense or wording. Have them share their free writing with you in order to bring voice to what they have written or drawn. Coach above-level students to write about higher-level concepts or processes. The more complex the concept, the more questions, concerns, and solutions will be generated. For below-level students, provide time for discussion before writing to build their confidence. Also allow these students to use pictures, words, phrases, etc., if necessary, instead of writing complete sentences and paragraphs.

Guided Free Write *(cont.)*

Grades 1–2 Example

Question:

Why is sharing important?

Student Free Write:

Sharing is important. It is nice to do. I like it when people share with me. It makes me feel good inside. Sometimes, I don't want to share with my little brother. I try to remind myself that I like it when he shares with me. So I should share with him. I don't mind sharing most of my toys. I don't like to share my favorite stuffed animal with him.

Grades 3–5 Example

Question:

Can two people with very different families and backgrounds be friends?

Student Free Write:

I think that people with different backgrounds can still be friends, but sometimes it is harder. Their families might not understand each other, and the parents might not like the kids playing together. Sometimes, people get scared of other people who are different. I think that is silly though because differences can make people special or interesting. My best friend Michael is a different religion from me, but we are still friends. We both like to play baseball and ride our bikes together even though we have different religions and backgrounds. I guess it depends how important the differences are to you.

Guided Free Write (cont.)

Grades 6–8 Example

Question:

What does the idiom *let sleeping dogs lie* mean? Do you agree with it?

Student Free Write:

The saying *let sleeping dogs lie* means that a person should not disturb the situation or else trouble will arise. I'm not sure if I agree with the idiom because I think it depends on the situation. In some cases, I think it is a good idea. For example, if I've been arguing with my sister and then we finally stop, it wouldn't be a good idea to bring up the conflict again. Sometimes, it is a good idea to bring up something bad though. If you see a person do something that you know is wrong, like break the law or hurt someone, it is always better to tell someone or call the police even if it means it might cause even more trouble.

Grades 9–12 Example

Question:

Is there such a thing as too much independence?

Student Free Write:

I think that too much independence can be a negative thing. Being independent means that you are not dependent on other people or things. Sometimes this can be helpful, like if you are independently wealthy and you don't need to rely on other people for income. But a certain amount of dependence is important because it is part of having relationships with other people. I think that if you are too independent, you'll end up isolated and lonely. Then again, if you are too dependent, that can cause problems too because you rely on other people for everything. I think some degree of dependence and independence is probably the best thing.

End-of-Class Reflection

Background Information

With the End-of-Class Reflection, students write on a notecard the three most important things learned from a reading assignment or activity, as well as two or three questions they want to ask about the central topic. This strategy meets many language arts classroom needs: students have an opportunity to summarize and paraphrase information, highlight main concepts, articulate their learning, and ask questions of the teacher. Teachers are able to quickly assess student understanding and analyze student reflections to direct future lessons. Research shows that writing about new knowledge is a key way to create lifelong learning.

Grade Levels/Standards Addressed

See page 63 for the standards this strategy addresses, or refer to the Digital Resource CD (standards.pdf) to read the correlating standards in their entirety.

Stage of Writing Process

Draft

Activity

At the end of a given lesson, instruct students to record three key things they learned during the lesson and three questions they still have about the topic. This activity can be completed in a student journal or on a 3" x 5" card that can be collected for teacher review.

Variation

For younger students who are still learning to write, consider recording students' dictated responses on the board. With upper grades, ask students to rank their key points in order of priority or emphasis. Then, lead a brief discussion at the end of class to review key concepts, analyze rankings, and discuss any questions that were raised.

Differentiation

Allow English language learners to write words or draw pictures to explain their key points or questions. Encourage them to get concepts down on paper and not worry about correct verb tense or wording. Expect above-level students to write more than three key points or to write an analysis of the learning they gathered from the lesson. Encourage these students to write questions that are open-ended, and encourage higher-level thinking. For below-level students, provide time—perhaps in a Think-Pair-Share—for discussion before writing. If students have an opportunity to discuss what they have learned, it will be easier for them to write. Model a sample response or simply the beginning of a sample response to show students how to get started. Then, ask them to use the model to write down their own thoughts.

End-of-Class Reflection (cont.)

Grades 1–2 Example

Learning:

A story's setting is where and when the story takes place.

A setting can be a geographic location, a physical location, or even a time period.

The author usually introduces the setting at the beginning of the book.

Questions:

What are different ways that an author can communicate setting to a reader?

How does a story's setting affect the plot?

Can a setting be an imaginary place?

Grades 3–5 Example

Learning:

An analogy is a comparison that shows the relationship between two things.

A metaphor is a direct comparison of two unlike things and does not use the words *like* and *as*.

A simile is a comparison of two unlike things and does use the words *like* and *as*.

Questions:

Why do authors use analogies in their writing?

Are metaphors and similes types of analogies?

How does an author choose to use a metaphor or a simile? Do they have different effects on the writing?

Grades 6–8 Example

Learning:

The theme of a story is the message the author wants to communicate to the reader.

The theme is related to a story's main ideas.

Some books have multiple themes.

Questions:

How do I determine the theme of a story?

Do authors decide on a theme before they start writing a story?

What is the difference between a theme and a moral?

End-of-Class Reflection (cont.)

Grades 9–12 Example

Learning:

There are many different types of narrators in fictional literature.

First- and third-person narrators are the most common.

An omniscient narrator knows the thoughts and feelings of one or more characters in the book.

Questions:

Is one type of narration more common than the others?

How does the type of narrator affect the tone of the story?

How can a reader discern whether a narrator is reliable?

Reader-Response Writing Chart

Background Information

The Reader-Response Writing Chart strategy, introduced by Allen Carey-Webb (2001), asks students to think about what they bring to a reading passage and what the author of the fictional text brings to the passage. When writing expository pieces, students need to try to remain neutral and focus on facts or research. In contrast, when writing persuasive pieces or narratives, students must establish a clear point of view or tone and communicate a theme to the reader. This strategy helps students become more aware of their biases and in what types of writing it is appropriate to use them. In fictional writing, the author's attitude is often expressed through the tone of the text, so this strategy gives students a tool for determining the tone of the text and deciphering how this tone relates to their own personal feelings or attitudes.

Grade Levels/Standards Addressed

See page 63 for the standards this strategy addresses, or refer to the Digital Resource CD (standards.pdf) to read the correlating standards in their entirety.

Stage of Writing Process

Draft

Activity

After reading a selected fictional text, distribute the *Reader-Response Writing Chart* activity sheet (page 83, readerresponse.pdf). On the left side, students write down the author's point of view on the topic. Require students to cite examples from the text to support their ideas. On the right side, students record the bias or attitude that they had going into the reading.

Discuss the following questions with students:

- What do you know about the subject?
- What are your feelings about this topic?
- Have you read anything about this subject before?
- What did you think about this subject?
- What tone does the author use in the text?
- Can you tell what he or she is thinking?
- Do you think the author has preconceptions about the topic?

In conclusion, ask students to record whether their views or opinions changed after completing the activity.

Variation

For primary grade classes, re-create the Reader-Response Writing Chart on the board or on a large sheet of chart paper. Lead a class discussion about each question and allow students to help formulate responses to add to the chart.

Reader-Response Writing Chart *(cont.)*

Differentiation

Encourage English language learners to work with partners when using this strategy to lower anxiety levels and promote collaboration. These students can record answers and share in the discussion. Challenge above-level students to identify multiple examples from the text to support their views of the author's bias and attitudes. Ask them to write about how these perspectives influence the author's writing. Take time to define and provide examples of bias and prejudice in a level-appropriate text for below-level students.

Grades 3–5 Example

The Author	Me
Her picky eating habits were only one example of her finicky personality traits. I think the author views picky eaters being difficult and fussy. Maybe he doesn't like that type of personality.	Just because a person is particular about one part of his or her life, like food, does not necessarily mean that he or she is picky about other things. I know plenty of people that do not like lots of different types of food, but they are not picky about the other things in their lives. I also know lots of people that are picky about other things, such as clothing, but will eat almost anything.

Grades 6–8 Example

The Author	Me
His lack of formal schooling made him ignorant to the rules of civilized society. The author seems to say formal schooling and social intelligence are the same.	While students do learn about social interactions in school, it is not the only place where people learn how to use good manners. It is very possible to have good manners without attending formal schooling. Furthermore, there are many people that have gone through years of formal schooling and yet know very little about manners or the rules for being around others.

Reader-Response Writing Chart (cont.)

Grades 9–12 Example

The Author	Me
The savagery of the natives excited my senses but weighed heavy on my conscience. There is no place for them in the modern world. It is important to distinguish between the author's point of view and the narrator's. This text tells me about the narrator's point of view.	When reading the text, I noted how the narrator uses opinionated vocabulary to describe the natives. It would be misleading to claim that these are the author's direct thoughts because there are multiple narrators. The text alternates between reliable and unreliable narrators, requiring me to pay particular attention to what is communicated through each narrator's telling. In this case, the narrator feels exhilarated by and pity for the natives. The narrator uses the word *savage* to convey the wild, primal side of humanity he observes in the natives. He also expresses the sadness he feels because he knows that the wild, primal nature of the natives cannot peaceably coexist in today's world.

Reader-Response Writing Chart

Directions: On the left side, write down the author's point of view on the topic. Also, note any examples of the author's attitude or biases. On the right side, record your own point of view regarding the subject.

The Author	Me

Story Impressions

Background Information

The Story Impressions strategy (McGinley and Denner 1987, as cited in Bintz 2011) helps motivate students to read a fictional text selection by arousing their curiosity and enabling them to make predictions about the story's characters, setting, and plot. The process of making predictions requires students to recall relevant information from prior experiences and integrate this information with their knowledge of story structure and literary elements. Prior to reading the selected text, students use a list of clue words or phrases taken directly from the text to develop an overall impression of the story. After reading, students compare their impressions with the original version of the story and note similarities and differences. The goal is not necessarily to have their information correct the first time but rather to activate prior knowledge, create a purpose for reading, examine information against a reliable source, and gain experience with determining and analyzing story structure.

Grade Levels/Standards Addressed

See page 63 for the standards this strategy addresses, or refer to the Digital Resource CD (standards.pdf) to read the correlating standards in their entirety.

Stage of Writing Process

Draft

Preparation

Prior to beginning the activity, create a chronological list of key words or phrases that will provide students with clues about the story's central elements. These words may relate to the story's characters, setting, or plot. Students should be able to use these words and phrases to write a general impression of the story.

Activity

To begin the lesson, distribute the prepared *Story Impressions* activity sheet (page 88, storyimpressions.pdf) to each student or display one on the board. Discuss the words and phrases on the list with students, clarifying definitions and providing context for the words as necessary. Encourage students to take notes about the words on their activity sheets. Once the class is familiar with the words and phrases, designate a set amount of time for them to complete the activity. There is no strict format to follow except that the clue words and phrases must be utilized. Allow time for students to share their Story Impressions with partners or table team for feedback and input. After reading the selected text, have students compare and contrast their Story Impressions with the text. This step is important because students are analyzing their own writing against published writing to verify information and develop metacognitive awareness about the learning process.

Story Impressions *(cont.)*

Differentiation

Provide clear, simple definitions and visuals of the key words for English language learners to refer to as they write their Story Impressions because it may be difficult for them to use the complex terms they have just learned. Provide sentence frames and examples of how to write a paragraph for English language learners as well. Instruct above-level students to incorporate additional words. For below-level students, spend individual time in a writing conference to work through the writing of the paragraph. Also, provide definitions for the key terms.

Story Impressions (cont.)

Grades 1–2 Example

Text: *One Morning in Maine* by Robert McCloskey

Clue Words and Phrases:

loose tooth	beach	sad	wish
father	lost	pillow	ice cream

Story Impression:

A child discovers that he or she has a loose tooth while she is at the beach with her father. The tooth falls out and gets lost. The child is very sad because she cannot put the tooth under her pillow and make a wish. The child makes a wish anyway and asks for ice cream.

How does your Story Impression compare to the text?

Some of my predictions were correct. Some were not. Sal already knew she had a loose tooth before she went down the beach. But the tooth did fall out and get lost there. Sal makes a secret wish that she will get ice cream. It comes true at the end of the story.

Grades 3–5 Example

Text: Chapter 1 in *Stuart Little* by E. B. White

Clue Words and Phrases:

mouse	human	helpful	drain
birth	strange	ring	

Story Impression:

A mouse gives birth to a strange human baby, and the baby turns out to be very helpful. He rescues a ring that falls down a drain.

How does your Story Impression compare to the text?

My ideas are mostly right, except a human mother gives birth to a mouse baby instead of the other way around. In the book, the baby, Stuart Little, is not strange, but the circumstances of his birth to human parents are very strange. He is a helpful mouse that rescues Mrs. Little's ring when it falls down a sink drain.

Story Impressions *(cont.)*

Grades 6–8 Example

Text: *A Lion to Guard Us* by Clyde Robert Bulla

Clue Words and Phrases:

brother	voyage	father	shipwreck
two sisters	ocean	tempest	island
stranded	colony	reunited	

Story Impression:

A brother and two sisters go on a voyage across an ocean to find their father. During the voyage, a tempest causes a shipwreck, leaving them stranded on an island. They discover a colony of native people living nearby, and they help reunite the children with their father.

How does your Story Impression compare to the text?

My summary is fairly accurate except for the part about the colony of native people. In this story, the colony is actually Virginia, one of the early American colonies, where the children are reunited with their father.

Grades 9–12 Example

Text: *The Book Thief* by Markus Zusak

Clue Words and Phrases:

World War II	traumatized	illiterate	Hitler's regime
10–year–old girl	death	bibliophile	book burning
foster family	brother	stolen books	Jewish refugee
hides	befriend	persecution	orphan

Story Impression:

The story takes place during World War II, when a 10-year-old girl goes to live with a foster family. She is traumatized by the death of her illiterate brother. Because of her brother's death, the girl becomes a bibliophile and collects stolen books. She does not understand when she sees Hitler's regime burning books, and she thinks they are books from the enemy. She befriends a Jewish refugee fleeing persecution, and her family hides the refugee to protect him. An intense episode of bombing kills everyone else in the girl's life, leaving her an orphan.

How does your Story Impression compare to the text?

The story does indeed take place during World War II and the main character, Liesel, is the bibliophile who is traumatized by her brother's death. However, it is Liesel, not her brother, who begins as illiterate and only learns to read as a result of help from her foster father, Hans. When Liesel witnesses Hitler's regime burning books, she makes Hitler her enemy and slowly begins to understand that he is responsible for the deaths of her brother and parents.

Story Impressions

Directions: Look at the list of words below and ask questions to clarify the meanings of any words that are unfamiliar to you. Then use the words in the order they are presented in the list to create and record your overall impression of what the story will be about.

Clue Words and Phrases:

_____   _____   _____

_____   _____   _____

_____   _____   _____

_____   _____   _____

_____   _____   _____

Story Impression:

_____

_____

_____

_____

_____

How does your Story Impression compare to the text?

_____

_____

_____

_____

Story Prediction Chart

Background Information

Students are typically more familiar with the content and story structure of narrative texts as opposed to expository texts, and this familiarity makes it easier for them to make predictions (Maria 1990). The Story Prediction Chart strategy is instrumental in helping students develop a purpose for reading by activating their prior knowledge about story structure and enabling them to make predictions based on visual information. In this strategy, students preview and discuss text features (e.g., title, cover, illustrations) in order to gather information to make predictions about the characters, events, and setting in the story. The teacher helps students recall information from their own experiences to help them form their predictions. Students record their predictions and the reasons that led them to their predictions before reading the story. Next, students read the text, stopping to confirm and revise their predictions as they proceed. After reading, students review their predictions, noting whether they were confirmed, and refer back to the story for textual evidence to support or refute their predictions. This part of the activity helps students learn how to draw evidence from literary texts to support the analysis of their predictions. Finally, students write a reflection about how the activity facilitated their comprehension of the story.

Grade Levels/Standards Addressed

See page 63 for the standards this strategy addresses, or refer to the Digital Resource CD (standards.pdf) to read the correlating standards in their entirety.

Stage of Writing Process

Draft

Activity

Begin the activity as a class to preview the upcoming reading selection. Show the text to students, and ask them to think about the cover illustration or picture, if applicable. For young students using picture books, take a picture walk through the book and make predictions based on the illustrations. Older students using chapter books can use the chapters in addition to the cover to form their predictions. Guide them to think about personal experiences or prior knowledge related to the topic. Use a document camera to display the *Story Prediction Chart* activity sheet (page 93, predictionchart.pdf) for students, or re-create it on the board. Record students' ideas and predictions on the chart. Have students read the text selection, or read it aloud to them. When about half of the text has been read, pause and ask students to review their predictions. *Have any of the predictions been confirmed? Do any of the predictions need to be revised? Do you want to add any new predictions about the second half of the story?*

Finish reading the text, and then return to the *Story Prediction Chart* activity sheet. Review the predictions, and note whether they were confirmed. Demonstrate how to refer back to the text to record the page number that contains the evidence for the response. Finally, ask students to

Story Prediction Chart (cont.)

write individual reflections on the ways in which this prediction strategy helped them improve their reading comprehension of the story.

Differentiation

For English language learners, make sure to define any new or challenging terms in the title of the story prior to beginning the activity. Make sure English language learners and below-level students have adequate time to process the visual information provided in the book during the preview. Above-level students should be encouraged to find multiple pieces of evidence that support or refute their predictions. Teach above-level students how to correctly quote directly from the text in order to provide evidence for their analysis.

Story Prediction Chart (cont.)

Grades 1–2 Examples

Text: *The Berenstain Bears' Sick Days* by Mike and Jan Berenstain

Predictions	Evidence/Reasons	Confirmed?	Page Number
Sister Bear gets sick.	Sister stays in bed, and Mama takes her temperature. That is what my mom does when I am sick.	Yes	9
Mama has to rush around taking care of Sister and Honey.	The illustrations show Mama doing lots of things for Sister and Honey at the same time.	Yes	11–12
Mama rests while Sister watches television.	Page 13 shows Mama sitting in a chair having a cup of tea. That is what my mom does when she needs a rest.	No	13
Sister makes a pretend catapult and knocks a plant off the table.	The illustrations on pages 17–18 show this happening.	Yes	17–18
By the end of the day, Sister is feeling better, but now Mama is sick.	Mama is holding her head in her hands and looks very tired. That is what I do when I am not feeling well.	Yes	25
Reflection			
I looked at pictures. They told me the answers. I listened more to find out if I was right. Now I know the story better. I went back and read it again. I wanted to know if I was right.			

Story Prediction Chart *(cont.)*

Grades 3–5 Examples

Text: *Beezus and Ramona* by Beverly Cleary, Chapter 1

Predictions	Evidence/Reasons	Confirmed?	Page Number
The story is about a younger sister and an older sister.	The front cover shows a picture of an older girl playing with a younger girl and they look similar. It also says *This little sister is impossible* on the cover. One of the chapters is called "Beezus and Her Little Sister," too.	Yes	1
The little sister likes to act wild and crazy.	In all of the illustrations, the little sister is doing something wild like riding her tricycle inside the house.	Yes	4
The first chapter takes place in the springtime close to Easter.	The little sister is wearing bunny ears in one illustration.	No	13 and 16
The older sister thinks the younger sister is annoying.	The older girl's facial expressions suggest that she thinks the younger girl is annoying. I know that I often think my younger sisters are annoying, too.	Yes	30
Reflection			
This activity made me think about my relationships with my younger sisters. I thought about how they annoy me a lot, but how I still like to do things with them sometimes. I'm curious to learn more about Beezus's relationship with her little sister, Ramona. By the end of the book, will Beezus be totally fed up with Ramona? Or will she see the benefits of having a younger sister? I think I paid more attention when I was reading because I wanted to know whether my predictions were correct.			

Story Prediction Chart

Directions: As you preview the book, record your predictions about the story. Note the reasons for your predictions. Once you have finished reading, note whether your predictions were confirmed in the text, and write down the page number where you found the evidence to refute or confirm your prediction. Reflect on your predictions and how they helped you comprehend the text in the bottom box.

Text: _____

Predictions	Evidence/Reasons	Confirmed?	Page Number
Reflection			

Journal Writing Overview

Benefits of Journal Writing

The quote "How do I know what I think until I see what I say?" by novelist E. M. Forster makes journal writing extremely relevant to students in the language arts classroom. Even in this crowded, technological world, there is still room for personal writing. Being able to express personal feelings in writing will always be vital to making sense of the world. Journal writing allows the writer to use words to express his or her understanding of literary concepts and to connect ideas from literature to his or her own life.

There are many benefits to using journal-writing strategies in the classroom. Journal writing provides a means for the student to absorb the complex themes presented in fictional narratives and record his or her reactions to new topics and ideas. Journal writing is a way for students to sort out all the new information and make sense of what they are learning. By writing in a daily journal, students become more comfortable with and confident in their writing and increase the number of words they are writing. This is another way for students to see their writing progress.

Journals mean different things to different educators, and they are used for a variety of purposes. However, the support for journal writing seems almost universal. Robert Yinger (1985, 31) states that "writing is a powerful tool for learning as well as for communicating."

How to Implement Journal Writing

Incorporating journal writing into the language arts classroom is easy because it does not take much class time and there is little or no teacher preparation. Journals do not need to be graded; the focus is on content, not on students' writing abilities or spelling, grammar, and punctuation skills. Be sure that students feel positive about writing each day in their journal. Do not make it seem like a punishment; your attitude as a teacher will mean everything.

Create or designate a journal for each student—and you—to use regularly. Students should date each entry so that it becomes a written record, documenting their growth and progress in learning. Be sure students have notebooks and pencils ready at journal time so that they can spend the entire time writing instead of looking for materials. Model good writing behavior by writing in your own journal.

Set aside a specific time each day during class for journal writing. Be sure to allow enough time for students to write a meaningful entry but not so much that it becomes boring and tedious. Select certain days throughout the week to have students share their journal entries with one another.

Journal Writing Overview (cont.)

Standards Addressed

The following chart shows the correlating standards for each strategy in this section. Refer to the Digital Resource CD (standards.pdf) to read the correlating standards in their entirety.

Strategy	McREL Standards	Common Core State Standards
Vocabulary Journal	Grades 1–2 (1.8) Grades 3–5 (1.5, 1.6) Grades 6–8 (1.5) Grades 9–12 (1.5, 1.6)	Grade 1 (CCRA.W.4, L.1.6) Grade 2 (CCRA.W.4, L.2.6) Grade 3 (W.3.4, L.3.6) Grade 4 (W.4.4, L.4.6) Grade 5 (W.5.4, L.5.6) Grade 6 (W.6.4, L.6.6) Grade 7 (W.7.4, L.7.6) Grade 8 (W.8.4, L.8.6) Grades 9–10 (W.9–10.4, L.9–10.6) Grades 11–12 (W.11–12.4, L.11–12.6)
Dialogue Journal	Grades 1–2 (1.6) Grades 3–5 (1.5, 1.10) Grades 6–8 (1.5) Grades 9–12 (1.5)	Grade 1 (CCRA.W.4, CCRA.W.10) Grade 2 (CCRA.W.4, CCRA.W.10) Grade 3 (W.3.4, W.3.10) Grade 4 (W.4.4, W.4.10) Grade 5 (W.5.4, W.5.10) Grade 6 (W.6.4, W.6.10) Grade 7 (W.7.4, W.7.10) Grade 8 (W.8.4, W.8.10) Grades 9–10 (W.9–10.4, W.9–10.10) Grades 11–12 (W.11–12.4, W.11–12.10)
Highlighted Journal	Grades 1–2 (1.1) Grades 3–5 (1.1, 4.1) Grades 6–8 (1.1, 4.3) Grades 9–12 (1.1)	Grade 1 (CCRA.W.7, CCRA.W.9) Grade 2 (CCRA.W.7, CCRA.W.9) Grade 3 (CCRA.W.9, W.3.7) Grade 4 (W.4.7, W.4.9) Grade 5 (W.5.7, W.5.9) Grade 6 (W.6.7, W.6.9) Grade 7 (W.7.7, W.7.9) Grade 8 (W.8.7, W.8.9) Grades 9–10 (W.9–10.7, W.9–10.9) Grades 11–12 (W.11–12.7, W.11–12.9)

Journal Writing Overview *(cont.)*

Strategy	McREL Standards	Common Core State Standards
Key Phrase Journal	Grades 1–2 (1.2) Grades 3–5 (1.2) Grades 6–8 (1.2) Grades 9–12 (1.2)	Grade 1 (CCRA.W.10, L.1.6) Grade 2 (CCRA.W.10, L.2.6) Grade 3 (W.3.10, L.3.6) Grade 4 (W.4.10, L.4.6) Grade 5 (W.5.10, L.5.6) Grade 6 (W.6.10, L.6.6) Grade 7 (W.7.10, L.7.6) Grade 8 (W.8.10, L.8.6) Grades 9–10 (W.9–10.10, L.9–10.6) Grades 11–12 (W.11–12.10, L.11–12.6)
Double-Entry Journal	Grades 3–5 (1.10, 1.11) Grades 6–8 (1.12) Grades 9–12 (1.12)	Grade 3 (W.3.8, W.3.10) Grade 4 (W.4.8, W.4.10) Grade 5 (W.5.8, W.5.10) Grade 6 (W.6.8, W.6.10) Grade 7 (W.7.8, W.7.10) Grade 8 (W.8.8, W.8.10) Grades 9–10 (W.9–10.8, W.9–10.10) Grades 11–12 (W.11–12.8, W.11–12.10)
Questioning Journal	Grades 3–5 (1.10, 1.11) Grades 6–8 (1.12) Grades 9–12 (1.12)	Grade 3 (CCRA.W.10, W.3.9) Grade 4 (W.4.9, W.4.10) Grade 5 (W.5.9, W.5.10) Grade 6 (W.6.9, W.6.10) Grade 7 (W.7.9, W.7.10) Grade 8 (W.8.9, W.8.10) Grades 9–10 (W.9–10.9, W.9–10.10) Grades 11–12 (W.11–12.9, W.11–12.10)

Vocabulary Journal

Background Information

The Vocabulary Journal provides an opportunity for students to communicate, and it can lead to self-reflection and growth. The Vocabulary Journal is an excellent resource to use with fictional literature because it allows students to write personally about the words they encounter in the text. The entries in a Vocabulary Journal vary—each one meets a specific need or skill. Expectations for the writing in the Vocabulary Journal vary according to students' levels. Through the continued use of Vocabulary Journals, students develop a comprehensive resource of many new general academic and domain-specific words that they can refer to for help with reading comprehension or writing.

Grade Levels/Standards Addressed

See page 95 for the standards this strategy addresses, or refer to the Digital Resource CD (standards.pdf) to read the correlating standards in their entirety.

Stage of Writing Process

Draft

Activity

Designate or create a notebook for each student to use as a Vocabulary Journal. This journal helps students keep track of and reflect on the many new words that are introduced in the study of fictional literature. Following is a variety of strategies to use with the Vocabulary Journal:

- Log new vocabulary words and their definitions as well as synonyms, antonyms, comparisons, etc.

- Write about the words students are learning. Ask students: *What has the experience been like? What have you learned? What do you hope to remember? What strategies can you use to retain these words? How does learning the meanings of words help you better understand literary concepts and information?*

- Explain the strategies that can be used when students encounter an unfamiliar word.

- Create a piece of fiction, such as a letter or a story, using the new vocabulary words.

- Write sentences using the vocabulary words.

- List the resources that are available for students to use when researching new vocabulary words.

- Design a journal entry to be shared with a partner or a small group.

Vocabulary Journal (cont.)

Variation

For primary grade students, create a class Vocabulary Journal. Allow students to dictate entries to be recorded by the teacher. This provides an opportunity for the teacher to model good writing skills. Or provide students with their own journals and allow them to draw and label pictures of vocabulary words. If students are able to use the word in a sentence or explain what it means orally, challenge them to write their response in their Vocabulary Journal.

Differentiation

Select Vocabulary Journal strategies that will encourage growth for English language learners but not overwhelm them, such as recording new vocabulary terms with their definitions, synonyms, and examples. Remind them to draw pictures to help create a visual connection. Challenge above-level students to write about complex literary terms in their Vocabulary Journals. Allow them to select words and entries that they are personally interested in. Limit the number of vocabulary words that below-level students write about. Provide them with sentence frames to help them meet the expectations of the assigned activity.

Vocabulary Journal (cont.)

Grades 1–2 Example

Vocabulary Words

1. **tryout:** when a person tries out for a part in a performance

   - synonyms: attempt, test

   - sample sentence: I hope I do well in my dance tryout next weekend.

2. **companion:** a person who is with another person

   - synonym: partner, pal, friend

   - sample sentence: My friend Nick is my companion because he likes to spend time with me.

3. **horrible:** when someone is mean or does mean things

   - synonyms: evil, bad, wrong

   - sample sentence: The horrible witch loved to cause trouble by scaring young children.

Grades 3–5 Example

simile: a comparison of two unlike things, using the words *like* or *as*

1. The truck was as big as a whale.
2. The wind whistled like a teakettle.
3. The sky was as black as coal.
4. My mouth felt as dry as dust.
5. The soap was as slippery as an eel.

metaphor: a direct comparison of two unlike things not using the words *like* or *as*

1. The man was a beast.
2. Time is money.
3. The market was a nightmare yesterday.
4. I am boiling mad.
5. She listened with a wooden face.

Vocabulary Journal (cont.)

Grades 6–8 Example

Dear Grace,

I'm writing to tell you about my <u>delightful</u> visit to the countryside during our vacation. The rolling greens hills made an <u>idyllic</u> setting for a restful <u>respite</u> from city life. We spent our days gathering wildflowers and observing the <u>multitude</u> of different types of birds. The food was absolutely <u>scrumptious</u>, too! We were sad that our little <u>sojourn</u> had to come to an end, but it is nice to be home now.

Your friend,

Emma

Grades 9–12 Example

When I encounter a word that is unfamiliar to me, there are a variety of different resources I can use to determine or clarify its meaning. A dictionary, either online or in book form, can provide information about a word's definition. A thesaurus can also be used to look up synonyms and antonyms for words. Dictionaries of root words contain information about the etymology of different words. The Internet contains a large number of resources, including online encyclopedias like Wikipedia that can be used to learn about new words, but it is important to verify the reliability of Wikipedia and other sources when using the Internet. People such as parents, teachers, and librarians, can also serve as resources.

Dialogue Journal

Background Information

A Dialogue Journal (Staton 1980) is just what the name implies—a dialogue between two or more people. Dialogue Journals can be shared between a student and a teacher or between one student and another student. This strategy does entail more work for teachers, but the dialogue exchange and extra effort is rewarding and informative. Using this strategy, teachers can recognize areas of student concern or misunderstanding with respect to the language arts content as well as student progress in communicating thoughts and ideas in writing. Students benefit from having an audience for their writing and using writing as an authentic form of communication. The Dialogue Journal provides an excellent place for students to practice casual writing for an informal audience.

Grade Levels/Standards Addressed

See page 95 for the standards this strategy addresses, or refer to the Digital Resource CD (standards.pdf) to read the correlating standards in their entirety.

Stage of Writing Process

Draft

Activity

Designate a notebook or binder to be used as the Dialogue Journal. Ask students to respond to a prompt or question, or occasionally allow them to write about a topic of their own. Using a combination of both adds variety to the strategy. Students then exchange Dialogue Journals with the teacher or a peer who then reads the journal entry and responds to questions or adds comments. Then, exchange again and write a new entry to continue the dialogue.

Variation

Create a teacher-class Dialogue Journal for primary grade students. Or provide a question or a prompt with a frame for the answer to assist these students.

Differentiation

Remind English language learners that this is a personal assignment, so they can respond in a way that is comfortable for them. Allow them to choose how they would like to communicate. Challenge above-level students by giving them specific feedback that will stimulate challenging thoughts and ideas and develop more effective writing skills. Encourage them to research ideas further and write about their findings in the next journal entry. When dialoguing with below-level students, be sure to keep your writing clear, concise, and easy to read. Use the journal as an opportunity to challenge their thinking even if the reading or writing skills are not high. Carefully consider whom to pair these students with when journals are exchanged.

Dialogue Journal (cont.)

Grades 1–2 Example

Student: I like the book *Lilly's Purple Plastic Purse*. It reminds me of my own life. Once, I brought a new toy to school. My kindergarten teacher took it away because I kept playing with it.

Teacher: I like the way you connected the story to your own life. How did your situation end? Do you think Mr. Slinger acted fairly when he took Lilly's purse away from her?

Student: I do think that Mr. Slinger acted fairly. He had already asked Lilly to put the purse away and she didn't listen. He gave her the purse back at the end of the day. That was nice of him. I don't really know why Lilly got so mad at Mr. Slinger.

Teacher: Try to put yourself in Lilly's shoes. She was really excited about her purse. Then Mr. Slinger took it away. Do you think the way she acted was really bad?

Student: I still don't understand why Lilly was so mad. I think her picture of Mr. Slinger wasn't nice. I do think that it was good that Lilly used writing to share her feelings.

Grades 3–5 Example

Student: I learned a lot about plot structure during the class discussion today. I understand the concepts of introduction, rising action, and conflict, but I'm confused about the climax. How do you determine the climax of a story?

Teacher: That's an excellent question. The climax is when the conflict in the story is finally resolved. So first, you have to identify the conflict in the story and then use that information to determine the climax.

Student: Okay, that makes sense. Now I'm confused about the falling action, though. I thought the conflict was resolved in the events in the falling action.

Teacher: The bulk of the conflict is resolved in the climax of a story. The purpose of the events that occur in the falling action after the climax is to tie up all the loose ends of the story and show how the resolution of the conflict affected various characters. I think it is great that you are thinking critically about plot structure. Keep up the good work!

Dialogue Journal *(cont.)*

Grades 6–8 Example

Student: Today, we talked about different types of figurative language and why authors choose to use them in their writing. I understand the concepts of simile and metaphor, but I still don't really understand their purpose. Doesn't the use of figurative language make writing more confusing for the reader?

Teacher: Figurative language is used in fiction to engage the reader and make the writing more interesting. While it might seem as if it would make the text more confusing, figurative language is often used to add emphasis so the reader can gain a better understanding of the text. For example, I could say, "The whale was big," or I could say, "The whale was as big as a bus." Which statement helps you understand my point better?

Student: I see what you are saying. By comparing a whale to a bus, you made me understand its size. Is figurative language mostly used to describe physical appearances?

Teacher: Actually, figurative language can be used to describe almost anything. In addition to physical objects, you can use figurative language to describe feelings, actions, or experiences. For instance, I could say, "My feet flew down the street," as a way of describing how fast I was running, even though feet can't really fly. Try to challenge yourself to use examples of figurative language the next time you write a narrative piece—you may find you enjoy it!

Grades 9–12 Example

Student: I noticed how Emily Brontë repeatedly mentions the landscape and the moors throughout *Wuthering Heights*. Does she do this for a reason?

Teacher: You made a good observation about the repeated appearance of the moors in *Wuthering Heights*. Usually authors spend a great deal of time, often years, writing novels of this length, so I believe that the majority of the text was carefully planned. What do you think? What role could the moors play in the story?

Student: I think the setting is symbolic because moors are open, boggy land that cannot be cultivated. This setting gives the story a sense of foreboding, especially because Brontë mentions the possibility of drowning in the moor several times throughout the book.

Teacher: I agree with you about the setting being symbolic. I think Brontë uses the moor as a setting to show how nature can be a threat. Do you think it is relevant that the moors are infertile? Do you think it is symbolic that Catherine and Heathcliff play on the moors as children? We're going to be discussing the setting of *Wuthering Heights* in class tomorrow, and if you feel comfortable, I think it would be great if you would share your insight with the rest of the class.

Highlighted Journal

Background Information

The Highlighted Journal is a strategy that assists students in making connections with their learning. Students need to regularly write about fictional literature in their journals for at least a month before trying this strategy. Students read through their journals and highlight key points—significant information or discoveries, points from class discussions, or concepts from a language arts text. They then use this information to build knowledge around a variety of concepts. This strategy helps develop research skills by asking students to analyze their written work for trends, commonalities, main ideas, themes, etc. By drawing evidence from their own texts, students can compile their learning to support the analysis and research of literary concepts.

Grade Levels/Standards Addressed

See page 95 for the standards this strategy addresses, or refer to the Digital Resource CD (standards.pdf) to read the correlating standards in their entirety.

Stage of Writing Process

Prewrite

Preparation

Have students routinely write about fictional literature in their journals for at least a month so that they will have enough writing to analyze for this strategy. Consider implementing the Journal-Writing strategies in this section to provide students with purposeful journal-writing activities in which students produce writing that can be analyzed for this strategy.

Activity

Tell students to read through their journals, looking for key words or concepts, common themes, or interesting points. Provide highlighters or allow students to use pencils to underline key points in their journal entries. Ask them to share their highlighted selections and the reasons why they chose them with each other or with the class.

Variation

For a primary grade class using a single journal between the teacher and the class, read through the journal entries together and ask students to identify the key points to highlight.

Differentiation

Prompt English language learners to look for common words that they see throughout their journals, as these are likely some of the key concepts and important vocabulary words that they need to know. Using this strategy serves as an effective review tool for them. Consider having above-level students explain to the class how they chose their highlighted points. For below-level students, take time to explicitly model how to identify significant information or common ideas in your own journal before asking them to apply the strategy.

Highlighted Journal (cont.)

Grades 1–2 Example

November 2

The <u>evil</u> <u>character</u> in the story is the witch. She tries to <u>trick</u> the <u>good</u> <u>character</u> named Sammy. She wants him to go into the woods alone.

November 3

The peddlers are the <u>bad</u> <u>characters</u>. They try to <u>fool</u> Joshua. They want him to <u>betray</u> his family.

November 4

If you are not fair, you will <u>not be happy</u>. That is the <u>point of the story</u>.

November 7

The <u>characters</u> show that being <u>kind is better than being evil.</u>

Grades 3–5 Example

February 10

At the <u>beginning</u> of the story, the reader learns about the characters, Henry and Harry, and that the story will <u>take place</u> on a <u>farm</u>.

February 11

I think the <u>setting</u> is very important to the story. It sets the <u>mood</u> as <u>dark</u> and <u>scary</u> even before the plot begins.

February 12

One way that the <u>author</u> <u>communicates</u> his <u>point of view</u> is through his choice of <u>setting</u>. By writing <u>about the beautiful landscapes in the Midwest, the author shows that he likes</u> open prairielands.

February 15

I think the story would be more interesting if it <u>took place</u> in <u>the future</u>. The author's <u>gloomy</u> and <u>negative</u> <u>attitude</u> shows that he <u>thinks</u> our current society is doomed to fail. He does not give any suggestions for changing this path. If he <u>set the story</u> in the future, then he could <u>suggest</u> ways to change the world rather than just accept the way it is.

Highlighted Journal (cont.)

Grades 6–8 Example

January 8

There are three types of <u>irony</u> in literature: <u>verbal</u>, <u>situational</u>, and <u>dramatic</u>.

January 11

When Uncle Scott says, "The water is as clear as mud," he is using <u>verbal irony</u> to indicate that the water was actually not clear at all. The use of irony in his speech <u>tells the reader</u> about Uncle Scott's <u>attitude</u> and <u>personality</u>—he is a very <u>sarcastic</u> character.

January 12

It is <u>ironic</u> that Mark's father, Steve, ends up writing for a travel magazine even though he rarely leaves his house and hates to travel. I think the author <u>included</u> this detail to <u>show</u> the reader that <u>life is not always clear</u> and sometimes <u>situations</u> turn out <u>differently than expected.</u>

Grades 9–12 Example

April 2

In *The Great Gatsby,* F. Scott Fitzgerald mentions a <u>green light</u> that Gatsby can barely see from his lawn. Is this light <u>symbolic</u>? What is its <u>purpose</u>?

April 7

Gatsby <u>associates</u> the <u>green light</u> with <u>Daisy</u> and <u>reaches out for it</u>. The <u>green light</u> seems to represent Gatsby's <u>dreams</u> or <u>desires</u>.

April 9

Since we know that Daisy loosely represents the American dream, the <u>green light</u> also seems to be a <u>symbol</u> for Gatsby's <u>dreams</u> about an <u>idealized future</u>. Later in the book, Nick <u>compares</u> the <u>green light</u> to how <u>America</u> must have seemed to the settlers when they first came to the new nation, again using the <u>green light</u> as a <u>symbol</u> for <u>hopes</u> and <u>dreams</u>.

Key Phrase Journal

Background Information

The Key Phrase Journal (Bringle and Hatcher 1996) is a strategy that assists students in regularly incorporating new academic vocabulary and phrases into their writing. During a language arts lesson, the teacher selects a list of literary terms or unknown vocabulary words students are to use in a journal entry. Through the process of incorporating these domain-specific words into their writing, students gain practice with accurately using the new terms in context. By using this strategy on a regular basis, students can develop a more solid understanding of the meanings of the new words and become more adept at using them consistently in their writing.

Grade Levels/Standards Addressed

See page 96 for the standards this strategy addresses, or refer to the Digital Resource CD (standards.pdf) to read the correlating standards in their entirety.

Stage of Writing Process

Draft

Activity

Prior to teaching a language arts lesson, make a list of words or phrases that students should understand thoroughly. These can be technical literary terms, such as hyperbole or simile, or general vocabulary drawn from the lesson's reading selection. Throughout the reading lesson or activity, introduce the words and use them in sentences or point them out in the text. Discuss the meanings of the words with students. After the lesson or later in the day, write the list of words and phrases on the board and instruct students to write an entry in their journals using those words.

Variation

With primary grade students, create sentences orally as a class. Write the sentences on the board or invite students to write them. To challenge upper grade students, let them select the words to incorporate into the journal entries, and ask them to persuade you to agree with their choices.

Differentiation

For English language learners, select from the list only the terms with which they are somewhat familiar—words that have been discussed as a class and defined on numerous occasions. Have them use only those words in their Key Phrase Journal so that they are not frustrated. Challenge above-level students to use words that are more difficult or less familiar to them by researching the terms and determining ways to incorporate them into the journal entry. For below-level students, allow them to select only one or two words to use in their journal entry and help them use resources to look up these words, if needed.

Key Phrase Journal (cont.)

Grades 1–2 Example

Key Words:

author, characters, setting

Journal Entry:

Authors are people who write stories. I can write a story. I can be an author. Stories have characters. And stories have settings. The characters are the people who the story is about. They do things together. They talk and make many choices. What the characters do is usually what the story is about. The setting is where the story happens.

Grades 3–5 Example

Key Words:

dusk, pesky, fetch, woodchuck

Journal Entry:

As dusk began to fall, the woodchuck poked his head out of an old stump and looked around. His short legs carried his round little body over to the garden fence where he hoped to fetch a few ripe vegetables for dinner. Just as he was about to grab a carrot, the pesky rabbit from the hollow log next door ran over and grabbed the carrot straight from his mouth. The woodchuck chased the rabbit, but it was no use—his short legs were no match for the rabbit's gigantic leaps.

from *Sarah, Plain and Tall* by Patricia MacLachlan

Key Phrase Journal (cont.)

Grades 6–8 Example

Key Words:

narrator, point of view, first person, third person, omniscient, peripheral, central

Journal Entry:

The narrator is the person who tells the story, and he or she can have different points of view. A first-person point of view means that the author is one of the characters in the story and tells the story from his or her perspective, using words like I or we. Third-person perspective is when the narrator is not a character in the story and tells the story from the view of an invisible observer. First-person narrators can be central, or main, characters in the story, or they can be peripheral, or minor, characters in the story. Third-person narrators can be omniscient, meaning that they know the thoughts and feelings of all the characters in the story, or limited omniscient, meaning that they only know the thoughts and feelings of one or more, but not all, characters.

Grades 9–12 Example

Key Words:

foreshadow, symbol, motif, theme

Journal Entry:

In *The Grapes of Wrath* by John Steinbeck, the theme of humankind's inhumane treatment of other humans plays an important role. Throughout the story, Steinbeck reinforces the idea that the hardship and suffering of the migrant workers stem mostly from the greediness of the landowners, not luck or the weather. The death of the Joad's dog when he is run over and then left for dead at a gas station foreshadows the hardships that await the Joads out West and symbolizes how humankind (driver of the car that killed the dog) will cause this suffering. Steinbeck also uses the motif of changing family structures to illustrate the power of family in the story. As Pa steps down from his role as the leader of the family, disrupting the traditional patriarchal family structure present at the beginning of the story, Ma steps up, taking on the untraditional leadership role of the family matriarch. Despite, or perhaps because of, this change in family structure, the power of the family endures and unites the Joads in their struggle for survival.

from *The Grapes of Wrath* by John Steinbeck

Double-Entry Journal

Background Information

The Double-Entry Journal (Angelo and Cross 1993) is a strategy to help students summarize what they read and to connect the reading with their own words and understanding. A Double-Entry Journal has two columns: one for notes, paraphrasing, and summaries; and the other for entries that express students' thoughts in their own words. This strategy allows teachers to immediately gauge student comprehension of the objectives and use that information in future lessons. It also focuses on the prewriting skills of note-taking and information analysis. Students analyze, synthesize, question, and write about what they are reading as well as personalize and reflect on what they have learned.

Grade Levels/Standards Addressed

See page 96 for the standards this strategy addresses, or refer to the Digital Resource CD (standards.pdf) to read the correlating standards in their entirety.

Stage of Writing Process

Prewrite

Activity

Before reading a selected fictional text, distribute the *Double-Entry Journal* activity sheet (page 113, doubleentry.pdf). On the left side, have students write notes or summaries of the reading, and on the right side, have them record personal reflections, observations, or questions. Select passages to focus on content or clarify misunderstandings, or allow students to select their own passages because of particular interests or questions they have about them.

When students have completed both sides of their journal entries, have them draw arrows to show the connections and relationships between the summary of the content and their personal thoughts and reflections. This reinforces for students what they are learning.

Differentiation

For English language learners, scaffold the activity by providing notes and key concepts for the left column in simple sentences that are easy to understand. Have these students read and discuss the notes before writing about them. Once they have written the personal reflection, suggest that English language learners draw arrows to show connections between the notes and their own words. Challenge above-level students to also write what they are thinking about as they write their notes. Another term for this is *thinking aloud*. Once the note-taking, summarizing, and thinking aloud are completed, have students write personal reflections. For below-level students, have them focus on only one or two key points to summarize from the lesson. Instruct them to keep their notes brief and limited so they can focus on their personal reflection without being overwhelmed by too many concepts to discuss.

Double-Entry Journal (cont.)

Grades 3–5 Example

Text: *Stone Soup* by Marcia Brown

Text Passage	Student Response
• Three hungry soldiers come to a town to ask for some food and a place to sleep. • The townspeople hide their food and say there is no place to sleep. • The soldiers declare that they will make stone soup from water and stones. • Gradually, the townspeople each give a little food to the soup. • The whole town has a feast. • The townspeople think the soldiers are very wise to be able to make soup from stones, so they give the soldiers the best beds in town. • The soldiers continue on their way.	• I like how the whole town ended up working together and contributing to make the soup. • I still don't understand if the townspeople understood that it was really them, not the soldiers, that actually created the soup.

Grades 6–8 Example

Text: *James and the Giant Peach* by Roald Dahl

Text Passage	Student Response
"At this point, James slowly put down his chopper and turned and looked across at the two women who were standing underneath the peach tree. *Something is about to happen*, he told himself. *Something peculiar is about to happen any moment.* He hadn't the faintest idea what it might be, but he could feel it in his bones that something was going to happen soon. He could feel it in the air around him . . . in the sudden stillness that had fallen upon the garden" (Dahl 19–20).	I think Roald Dahl uses James's thought that something peculiar is going to happen to foreshadow upcoming events in the story. Like James, I don't know what will happen, but it makes me excited to keep reading the book. I think that this type of foreshadowing is interesting because the reader doesn't know if the upcoming event will be positive or negative.

Double-Entry Journal *(cont.)*

Grades 9–12 Example

Text: *The House on Mango Street* by Sandra Cisneros

Text Passage	Student Response
The chapter "My Name" in *The House on Mango Street* by Sandra Cisneros tells how Esperanza does not like her name. Even though it means "hope," Esperanza thinks that it has too many letters and, in her view, it means "sadness" and "waiting" (Cisneros 10–11).	This chapter made me feel sad. Esperanza seems to really hate her name, even though it signifies something beautiful. Maybe Esperanza's feelings about her name symbolize her lack of hope about her future, since her name means "hope." Or maybe she feels like her parents have very high hopes for her since they gave her that name and she is worried about not meeting these expectations. I hope we learn more about Esperanza and her relationship with her name in upcoming chapters.

Name: _____   **Date:** _____

Double-Entry Journal

Title: _____

Text Passage	Student Response
• Write the passage directly from the text. • Write notes from the text. • Write a summary of a section of text.	• What are your reactions to the text? • What does it remind you of? • What questions do you still have?

Questioning Journal

Background Information

Journals allow students to reflect on their reading, leading to better classroom discussions and increased comprehension (Maria 1990). Journal writing allows students to integrate their knowledge of reading and writing so they can see how each skill can be used to support the other. In the Questioning Journal, students record their questions about the reading as they arise and then note any answers or relevant information about their questions as they continue reading. This strategy is similar in format to the Double-Entry Journal strategy, but the emphasis is on questioning rather than summarizing. The Questioning Journal is used before, during, and after a reading so that students can record their questions as they occur and also draw evidence from the text to provide answers to their questions and material for further reflection.

Grade Levels/Standards Addressed

See page 96 for the standards this strategy addresses, or refer to the Digital Resource CD (standards.pdf) to read the correlating standards in their entirety.

Stage of Writing Process

Draft

Activity

Distribute the *Questioning Journal* activity sheet (page 117, questioning.pdf) to students before beginning the reading selection. Instruct students to record their questions about the text in the left-hand column and their thoughts, answers, or other information relevant to their questions in the right-hand column. If appropriate, the teacher may choose to narrow the scope of students' questions in order to focus on specific literary elements. For example, a teacher might ask students to record their questions concerning the characters in the story and how they develop over the course of the text. Encourage students to take the time to stop and record their questions as they occur rather than reading on in hopes that the text will answer the questions.

Differentiation

For English language learners, provide a list of sample questions to help guide their thinking and writing for the left-hand column. Encourage them to complete the reflection and analysis independently, asking for assistance from the teacher or their peers when necessary. Below-level students will benefit from a shorter text selection. These students may have an abundance of questions, so help them choose several important ones to focus on. Multiple readings of the text selection will also help them draw the relevant information from the text to answer their questions. Above-level students should be instructed to ask more complex questions rather than simpler, factual questions about the text. Guide them in developing questions about literary concepts such as theme, symbolism, and imagery that will deepen their reading comprehension.

Questioning Journal (cont.)

Grades 3–5 Example

Text: *Charlotte's Web* by E. B. White

Questions	Relevant Information/Answers
Why did Mr. Arable want to kill Wilbur?	Mr. Arable was going to kill Wilbur because he was the runt of the litter, but I'm still not sure what *runt* means.
What does the word *runt* mean?	The runt is the smallest animal in the litter. The runt of a litter is often weak and sometimes does not survive for very long. Mr. Arable thought Wilbur would die anyway.
Why did Wilbur have to go live with the Zuckermans?	Mr. Arable still sees Wilbur as something to be bought and sold, not as a pet, and he is concerned that Fern will get too attached to Wilbur. They compromise by selling Wilbur to Fern's uncle down the road.

Grades 6–8 Example

Text: *Of Mice and Men* by John Steinbeck

Questions	Relevant Information/Answers
Why does George stick with Lennie after Lennie gets them in trouble at the last farm where they worked?	George has assumed the responsibility to care for Lennie, and he sees Lennie as his friend. Lennie and George are united by a common dream of owning their farm with a house and a rabbit hutch.
What is the significance of Candy's dog in the story?	Candy loves his old dog although he cannot voice these feelings. In the end, he lets Carlson shoot his dog, but then Candy wonders whether he should have done it himself. Candy's relationship with his dog seems to parallel George's relationship with Lennie.
How could George shoot Lennie at the end of the story?	George shot Lennie to save him from Curly's lynch mob. He knew that Lennie would experience nothing but suffering after he killed Curly's wife, and he wanted to save him from that. George knew that Lennie depended on him, so he had to do what he thought would limit Lennie's suffering.

Questioning Journal (cont.)

Grades 9–12 Example

Text: *The Kitchen God's Wife* by Amy Tan

Questions	Relevant Information/Answers
What is the relationship between Helen and Winnie?	Although they are not blood sisters, they act just like siblings. They have huge fights, but they also share a very special and deep bond. Helen is the only person that knows Winnie's real story.
Why does Winnie keep cleaning her house?	Winnie starts to clean when she wants to forget something from her past. It seems like she uses it as a distraction from things she does not want to think about or remember.
Why does Winnie hide in her aunts' greenhouse?	When Winnie goes to live with her aunts, she feels out of place and unwanted. Her uncle built the greenhouse so he could practice a western hobby, gardening. When he got bored with gardening, the greenhouse just became a storage shed. Winnie finds a painting of her mother in the greenhouse, giving the location special significance.

Name: _____ **Date:** _____

Questioning Journal

Text: _____

Questions	Relevant Information/Answers

Note-Taking Overview

Note-taking is a crucial skill for students in upper-elementary grades and beyond. High school and college students do a significant amount of note-taking during classes and while reading, so it makes sense for this skill to be taught to our younger students, as well. Teachers often ask students to take notes or copy modeled notes during a lecture. Some ask for notes as evidence of completing assigned independent reading. Additionally, notes can be useful as a review tool before an assessment.

Note-taking is also an important research skill, as it provides a system for organizing information. As students read various research sources, they must extract the larger overarching ideas and the supporting details. If students are to apply this information in a meaningful way, they must arrange the information in such a way that makes sense. Otherwise, the notes are simply a laundry list of random information. By providing instruction on effective note-taking systems, teachers can help their students become more efficient researchers.

It is important to note that this skill needs to be taught with a clear explanation, teacher modeling, guided practice, and explicit feedback. As with any other strategy, students must reach a level of proficiency before they are expected to use the strategy independently. Teachers can employ the same instructional strategies that are effective when teaching other skills: display the selection with a document camera, conduct a think-aloud as the main ideas and details are identified, model how to use the designated note-taking strategy on chart paper or with a document camera, and ask for student assistance to complete the notes. Upper-elementary students may need the notes scaffolded for them, with some of the information filled in, in order to develop a useful set of notes.

Teachers can make the connection between reading and writing explicit by discussing how text structures are mirrored between the two. Students who are familiar with various text structures will be better able to learn and use the note-taking strategies. For example, a narrative text with several prominent themes may lend itself well to a strategy such as a T-List, where main ideas are listed in one column and the corresponding details are listed in the other. Additionally, a fictional text that describes a series of events may be better suited to the Note-Taking System for Learning, where each event has a section within the outline. Teachers may want to introduce one of these strategies immediately following a reading lesson on main idea or plot sequence. In this way, teachers can provide an authentic opportunity for students to apply that "reading" skill to a "writing" strategy.

To extend the value of note-taking, teachers can show students how to use their notes to apply new knowledge to a writing activity. Well-organized notes are an excellent foundation for a well-written assignment. Teachers can remind students to make use of their notes to begin a piece of writing, as they serve as an effective prewriting strategy. Again, this can show students the connection between reading and writing.

Note-Taking Overview (cont.)

Standards Addressed

The following chart shows the correlating standards for each strategy in this section. Refer to the Digital Resource CD (standards.pdf) to read the correlating standards in their entirety.

Strategy	McREL Standards	Common Core State Standards
Cornell Note-Taking System	Grades 3–5 (4.7) Grades 6–8 (4.5) Grades 9–12 (4.6)	Grade 3 (W.3.8) Grade 4 (W.4.8) Grade 5 (W.5.8) Grade 6 (W.6.8) Grade 7 (W.7.8) Grade 8 (W.8.8) Grades 9–10 (W.9–10.8) Grades 11–12 (W.11–12.8)
Note-Taking System for Learning	Grades 3–5 (4.7) Grades 6–8 (4.5) Grades 9–12 (4.6)	Grade 3 (W.3.8) Grade 4 (W.4.8) Grade 5 (W.5.8) Grade 6 (W.6.8) Grade 7 (W.7.8) Grade 8 (W.8.8) Grades 9–10 (W.9–10.8) Grades 11–12 (W.11–12.8)
T-List	Grades 3–5 (4.7) Grades 6–8 (4.5) Grades 9–12 (4.6)	Grade 3 (W.3.8) Grade 4 (W.4.8) Grade 5 (W.5.8) Grade 6 (W.6.8) Grade 7 (W.7.8) Grade 8 (W.8.8) Grades 9–10 (W.9–10.8) Grades 11–12 (W.11–12.8)
Sticky Note Annotation System	Grades 3–5 (4.7) Grades 6–8 (4.5) Grades 9–12 (4.6)	Grade 3 (CCRA.W.9, W.3.8) Grade 4 (W.4.8, W.4.9) Grade 5 (W.5.8, W.5.9) Grade 6 (W.6.8, W.6.9) Grade 7 (W.7.8, W.7.9) Grade 8 (W.8.8, W.8.9) Grades 9–10 (W.9–10.8, W.9–10.9) Grades 11–12 (W.11–12.8, W.11–12.9)

Cornell Note-Taking System

Background Information

The Cornell Note-Taking System (Pauk 1988) strategy teaches students how to effectively take notes during a language arts lecture. This strategy teaches students to take clean notes and to organize the notes for the best study options later. The Cornell Note-Taking Strategy encourages students to summarize important points while they take notes and then categorize this information into main ideas and details. It requires a lot of practice time for students. Teach the Cornell Note-Taking System by modeling or practicing each day and slowly incorporating the different stages of the system.

Grade Levels/Standards Addressed

See page 119 for the standards this strategy addresses, or refer to the Digital Resource CD (standards.pdf) to read the correlating standards in their entirety.

Stage of Writing Process

Prewrite

Activity

Create or designate a notebook for the *Cornell Note-Taking System* activity sheet (page 122, cornellsystem.pdf) so that sheets can be added or removed. Instruct students to write on only one side of the paper. The right-hand side is the Notes column for notes taken during the lecture. The left-hand side is the Recall column, where key words or phrases that summarize the notes

are recorded. Before beginning a lecture, explain that students should focus on the Notes column. Remind students that they should paraphrase the information and not try to write down their notes verbatim. Encourage them to use abbreviations or phrases and to write down the big ideas when taking notes. Students may need to skip lines to leave room for adding information later. Discuss the notes from the lecture and the different ways that students can record this information. Remind students to focus on the main ideas and key terms of the content and to not get bogged down with too many details. After the lecture, instruct students to read through their Notes and write down key points or terms in the Recall column. These key words or phrases will help them recall the main idea of each section of notes without having to read through the whole Notes section. Remind students to review their notes each day to place the information into long-term memory.

Variation

When students are finished, have them use their Notes to write questions about the material that might be asked on future tests. Or instruct students to cover up the Notes side and use the cue words on the Recall side to describe the details of each concept. Students can verify what they have recited by uncovering the Notes column and checking their work.

Differentiation

When working with English language learners, scaffold the Notes page by providing some of the main ideas to help these students preview the information and shape their focus for the lecture. Challenge above-level students to add diagrams, maps, and charts in the notes column to visually portray important concepts. For below-level students, preview the main ideas of the lecture and explain how to identify important as well as extraneous information. This discussion will help these students organize and understand their notes and cement information taught during the lecture.

Cornell Note-Taking System *(cont.)*

Grades 3–5 Example

Topic: inferences

Recall	Notes
Inferences are conclusions draws from the text. Inferences are not obvious or stated in the text. Inferences help the reader understand the text better.	• readers make inferences by combining information in the text with personal background knowledge or experiences • readers have to make inferences to understand main ideas or themes • inferences are not ideas or facts stated outright in a text • readers make inferences about characters' thoughts, opinions, and actions • inferences can also be thought of as conclusions drawn from the text

Grades 6–8 Example

Topic: Greek or Latin root words

Recall	Notes
Greek and Latin root words can help the reader understand the meaning of new vocabulary words. Words that share common roots often have similar definitions.	• many of our words in the English language come from Greek or Latin • Greek and Latin roots help the reader understand the meaning of new words • words that share common Greek or Latin roots often share similar meanings • learning about root words helps you understand the origin of the word and how it came to have its present-day meaning • root words can be combined with knowledge about prefixes and suffixes to determine meaning

Grades 9–12 Example

Topic: hyperbole

Recall	Notes
Hyperboles are figures of speech that use exaggeration to communicate a point. Hyperboles are often used for emphasis but can also be used to add humor to writing. Hyperboles help the reader visualize or imagine a certain aspect of the story.	• an exaggerated figure of speech • not meant to be taken literally • can be used to add humor to the text • makes writing more engaging for the reader • used to communicate a point indirectly • used to create imagery • helps the reader visualize the character, setting, or situation • often used with similes and metaphors when comparing two unlike things

Cornell Note-Taking System

Directions: During a lecture, take notes in the Notes column, using short phrases and abbreviations. After the lecture, review your notes and write the key points in the Recall column.

Topic: _____

Recall	Notes

Note-Taking System for Learning

Background Information

Students in the upper-elementary, middle, and high school grades are required to take notes on lectures and presentations. Often, students do not have experience with or the understanding of how to take notes, and the Note-Taking System for Learning strategy (Palmatier 1973) helps them learn this valuable skill. By using this strategy, students learn how to gather, categorize, and organize relevant information in a useful and efficient manner. Note-taking allows students to accurately and efficiently summarize information from the text in order to improve reading comprehension and reinforce new learning.

Grade Levels/Standards Addressed

See page 119 for the standards this strategy addresses, or refer to the Digital Resource CD (standards.pdf) to read the correlating standards in their entirety.

Stages of Writing Process

Prewrite

Activity

Before introducing this strategy, distribute the *Note-Taking System for Learning* activity sheet (page 126, notesystemlearning.pdf) to students. The strategy has three main components:

1. **Recording**—During a lecture, have students write down the main ideas and supporting details in outline form. Instruct them to leave space between main ideas as needed for future notes and additions. Robert Palmatier suggests writing only on the front of the pages to avoid confusion later. Model for students how to take notes; after reading a passage from a text, take notes on a chart or use a document camera to show how to choose the key points. Give students plenty of practice taking notes before expecting them to do it independently.

2. **Organizing**—When students have completed their notes, have them number the pages and staple them in order. Next, have students read through their notes and add labels in the left margin that describe the gist of the notes. This allows time for students to review what they have written and helps them identify any confusion they may have about the content. Students may also add to their notes, incorporating information from the text, lecture, or additional research that clarifies existing information. Use the blank side of the paper for this.

3. **Studying**—Once students have organized all the information in one place, instruct them to use their notes to study. The labels and information in the left margin provide a summary and overview of their notes.

Differentiation

Scaffold notes for English language learners by providing them with the main points. Then, have them focus on adding details during the note-taking process. They will still have the opportunity to summarize and label their notes in the left margin. Challenge above-level students to add to their notes by reading other texts related to the topic. Be sure the new materials are at a challenging reading level. For below-level students, clearly define main ideas and details and provide examples of completed notes pages. Prior to the lecture, provide them with the main ideas so that they can listen for and record the details.

Note-Taking System for Learning *(cont.)*

Grades 3–5 Example

Subject: plot sequence

I. Introduction

    a. Kenny and his family live in Flint, Michigan.

    b. Kenny's family members are his dad, mom, older brother Byron, and younger sister Joetta.

II. Rising Action

    a. Byron becomes friends with Buphead, and they start getting into trouble together.

    b. Kenny's parents decide that the family is going to take a trip to Alabama to visit Grandma Sands. Kenny will have to stay there if he cannot change his behavior.

III. Climax

    a. Grandma Sands's church is bombed. Everyone think that Joetta was at the church when the bombings occurred.

    b. Joetta turns out to be safe because she left the church before the bombing.

IV. Falling Action

    a. The family immediately leaves Birmingham and goes back to Michigan.

    b. Kenny struggles to understand the church bombing.

V. Resolution

    a. Byron helps Kenny work through his feelings about the bombing by showing him that he is not to blame for what happened.

from *The Watsons Go to Birmingham–1963* by Christopher Paul Curtis

Note-Taking System for Learning (cont.)

Grades 6–8 Example

Subject: theme of dedication

I. Billy

    a. Billy shows determination by saving his money for two years to buy his dogs.

    b. He walks through the forest by himself at night to get the dogs.

    c. He labors hard to cut down the big sycamore tree so his dogs will not feel let down.

    d. He shows determination when he wins the coon-hunting championship.

II. Old Dan and Little Anne

    a. The dogs are always extremely determined to catch raccoons.

    b. As their relationship with Billy evolves, the dogs also become determined to not let Billy down.

from *Where the Red Fern Grows* by Wilson Rawls

Grades 9–12 Example

Subject: symbolism of fire

I. Fire is symbolic of Okonkwo's physical anger.

    a. Fire destroys everything it consumes.

    b. Okonkwo physically kills Ikemefuna and Ogbuefi Ezeudu's son.

II. Fire is symbolic of Okonkwo's psychological destructiveness.

    a. Anger is the only emotion Okonkwo permits himself to display.

    b. Okonkwo eventually succumbs to the fire, or rage, inside of him, and it destroys him.

from *Things Fall Apart* by Chinua Achebe

Note-Taking System for Learning

Directions: During a lecture, write down the main ideas and supporting details in outline form.

Subject: _____

I. _____

    a. _____

    b. _____

    c. _____

    d. _____

II. _____

    a. _____

    b. _____

    c. _____

    d. _____

III. _____

    a. _____

    b. _____

    c. _____

    d. _____

T-List

Background Information

The T-List strategy (Chamot and O'Malley 1994; Hamp-Lyons 1983) organizes information into main ideas and details. It is also an effective alternative to quizzes and short-answer tests for assessing student comprehension. This strategy can facilitate question-and-answer discussions and oral summaries. The T-List is a visual representation of information that students can use to write about a given topic. This strategy is effective for taking notes on both lectures and reading selections. When taking notes while reading, students should also be taught how to cite their literary sources and provide a list of sources to enhance credibility and avoid plagiarism.

Grade Levels/Standards Addressed

See page 119 for the standards this strategy addresses, or refer to the Digital Resource CD (standards.pdf) to read the correlating standards in their entirety.

Stage of Writing Process

Prewrite

Activity

Distribute the *T-List* activity sheet (page 129, tlist.pdf) to students or have them create their own by drawing a large *T* on a blank sheet of paper. On the left side of the T-List, students list main ideas or key concepts from the reading passage or lecture. On the right side of the T-List, students record the corresponding details that support the main ideas. Explain to students that they will organize the main ideas and details of a fictional text or language arts lecture on the chart. As the lesson proceeds, help students identify the main ideas and demonstrate how to write them in the left-hand column, using two or three words. Students should then write the corresponding details in their own words, rather than copy them from the text, in the right-hand column. Make sure to demonstrate how to accurately cite the text from which the notes are drawn and teach students how to compile a list of sources using a standard format for citation.

Differentiation

Fill in portions of the T-List prior to giving it to English language learners, and have them identify supportive details as they read. Also, be sure to preteach any challenging vocabulary words they might encounter. Challenge above-level students with the T-List by assigning a chapter, and have students create and fill in a T-List independently. Organize them in a small group to compare their T-Lists and justify their decisions. For below-level students, provide the main ideas for the left-hand column as a scaffold.

T-List (cont.)

Grades 3–5 Example

Subject: *The Secret Garden* by Frances Hodgson Burnett

Main Ideas	Details
positive thinking leads to physical health negative effects of secrets	Mary begins to explore the gardens → develops positive thinking and imagination → physical health improves Colin's change in attitude and way of thinking → develops physical improvement Colin is kept secret from the world → his health continues to deteriorate Mary's parents kept her secret from their associates in India the garden is secret Misselthwaite is full of secret rooms and a secret history disclosure of these secrets → leads to positive thinking and increased happiness

Grades 6–8 Example

Subject: personification

Main Ideas	Details
occurs when a writer gives an inanimate object human traits or qualities used to help describe objects, feelings, events, or ideas	helps readers comprehend ideas better can be used to add emphasis can be used to describe the physical aspects of objects—"the house looked depressed" can be used to describe actions: "the stars were dancing in the sky" makes writing more interesting and helps engage the reader

Grades 9–12 Example

Subject: point of view

Main Ideas	Details
First person point of view—can be central or peripheral Third person point of view—can be limited omniscient or omniscient	first-person point of view is when the narrator is a character in the story first-person central is when the narrator is one of the main characters first-person peripheral is when the narrator is not a main character in the story third-person point of view is when the narrator is not a character in the story an omniscient point of view is when the narrator "knows everything," including the thoughts and feelings of all characters a limited-omniscient narrator knows the thoughts and feelings of one or more characters but not all of the characters

Name: _____ **Date:** _____

T-List

Directions: Write the main ideas gained from the reading or lecture in the left-hand column. Then, add details that support each main idea in the column on the right.

Main Ideas	Details

Sticky Note Annotation System

Background Information

Children are often reprimanded not to write in books, yet it is this urge to dynamically interact with the text that helps develop reading comprehension as they grow older (Dingli 2011). Note-taking allows the reader to summarize important points, ask questions, highlight points of confusion, make connections between ideas, and analyze key concepts in the reading. The Sticky Note Annotation System enables students to take notes directly in the book by writing them on sticky notes and fixing them directly onto the text. Students can use the sticky notes in the text to review the reading material and gather main ideas from the selection. The sticky notes can also be removed and reorganized to create a study guide, develop an outline, identify themes, or support research.

Grade Levels/Standards Addressed

See page 119 for the standards this strategy addresses, or refer to the Digital Resource CD (standards.pdf) to read the correlating standards in their entirety.

Stage of Writing Process

Prewrite

Activity

Distribute a set of sticky notes to each student, cutting them in half if necessary to create the appropriate size for a note. Display a copy of the reading selection with a document camera, or at least use the beginning of the text, and ask students to take turns reading sections aloud. Periodically stop students and use a think aloud to model your thought process for making a note about something in the text. Write your note on a sticky note, and stick it directly on the text in the appropriate location. Continue reading the text aloud, placing notes where appropriate. Allow students to finish the text independently, making their own notes on sticky notes and attaching them to the text. When they are finished, have students compare their notes with a classmate's. Finally, model some of the ways students can use their sticky notes to support analysis, reflection, and research.

Differentiation

English language learners may benefit from completing this activity with a partner to ensure accurate comprehension of the text selection. For below-level students, make several observations on sticky notes that highlight main ideas or important points in the text for them. Allow them to place these notes on the text when they come across the appropriate location in the text. It may be helpful to provide these readers with a shortened or leveled reading selection to assist with reading comprehension. Above-level students should be challenged to use their sticky notes to analyze more complex elements or literary concepts of the text, such as theme and symbolism.

Sticky Note Annotation System *(cont.)*

Grades 3–5 Example

Text: *Freckle Juice* by Judy Blume

Passage:

"[Andrew] sat in class all day with his blue freckles. A couple of times Miss Kelly looked at him kind of funny but she didn't say anything. Then at two o'clock she called him to her desk.

'Andrew,' Miss Kelly said. 'How would you like to use my secret formula for removing freckles?' Her voice was low, but not so low that the class couldn't hear" (Blume 35–36).

> Andrew's teacher knows something isn't right, but she doesn't say anything right away.

> Miss Kelly is trying to save Andrew from further embarrassment. She is his ally in this situation.

Grades 6–8 Example

Text: *The Chocolate Touch* by Patrick Skene Catling

Passage

"While other boys and girls spent their money on model airplanes, magazines, skipping ropes, and pet lizards, John studied the candy counters. All his money went on candy, and all his candy went to himself. He never shared it. John Midas was candy mad" (Catling 4).

> Earlier in the book, the author writes that, "[John] had one bad fault: he was a pig about candy." His lack of sharing seems like another bad, or perhaps even worse, fault to me.

> John's last name is Midas. I think that is a reference to the Greek god Midas, who had the ability to turn everything he touched into gold.

Sticky Note Annotation System (cont.)

Grades 9–12 Example

Text: *Fahrenheit 451* by Ray Bradbury

Passage:

"It was a special pleasure to see things eaten, to see things blackened and *changed*. With the brass nozzle in his fists, with this great python spitting its venomous kerosene upon the world, the blood pounded in his head, and his hands were the hands of some amazing conductor playing all the symphonies of blazing and burning to bring down the tatters and charcoal ruins of history" (Bradbury 3).

The narrator describes burning as "a special pleasure," yet he uses the frightening imagery of a venomous snake to describe it. What does the narrator truly believe or feel about fire?

Another example of how the author writes about fire as good ("his hands were the hands of some amazing conductor") and evil ("bringing down the tatters and charcoal ruins of history").

Maybe Bradbury is trying to explain to the reader how his futuristic society views things like fire (positive) and history (negative) while also communicating his personal beliefs about the detrimental aspects of these views.

Frame *(cont.)*

Grades 9–12 Example

Topic: figurative language

Type of Figurative Language	Role in Story	Description
simile	a comparison between two unlike things, using the words *like* or *as*	The man was as tall as a skyscraper.
metaphor	a comparison between two unlike things and not using the words *like* or *as*	He was a feather on the wind floating gracefully across the stage.
personification	giving inanimate objects human traits or qualities	The party died as soon as he left.
hyperbole	exaggerated statement not meant to be taken literally	I have a ton of homework.
alliteration	using words that begin with the same letter or sound consecutively or close together	The soft sun swept over the sand.
onomatopoeia	the use of words that imitate the sounds associated with the objects or animals that the word references	"Meow!" screeched the cat.
idiom	an expression that means something other than the literal meaning of the words	It is raining cats and dogs.

Name: _____ **Date:** _____

Frame

Directions: Write in the topic for the Frame and the titles for each column. Then, fill in each box with information from the text.

Topic: _____

Conflict-Resolution Map

Background Information

A Conflict-Resolution Map is a graphic organizer that helps organize information about the central conflict in a narrative and the way it is resolved throughout the story. The Conflict-Resolution Map encourages students to analyze the plot, identify the conflict during the rising action sequence of events, and summarize how the conflict is resolved in the climax and falling-action portions of the story. Students can then use this strategy to organize information for different aspects of the text or to compare a particular text to another.

Grade Levels/Standards Addressed

See page 134 for the standards this strategy addresses, or refer to the Digital Resource CD (standards.pdf) to read the correlating standards in their entirety.

Stage of Writing Process

Prewrite

Activity

Prior to reading a specific fictional text selection, explain to students that they will be analyzing the conflict and solution in the story. If needed, define the terms *conflict* and *resolution* and provide examples, especially for students in the primary grades. Distribute the *Conflict-Resolution Map* activity sheet (page 148, conflictresolution.pdf) to students, and explain how to use it.

- Ask questions that can help identify the conflict(s): *What happens or changes the situation? What is the problem in the story? What are the characters working to solve?* Once students have identified the conflict, have them write a description of it. The more descriptive they are, the better they will be able to identify the solution.

- Ask questions that can help students identify the resolution(s): *What is the result of the conflict? What happened after the conflict? How did the characters solve the main problem?* Make sure that students identify all the resolutions, even if there is more than one resolution. Encourage them to think about any resolutions that may not be obvious.

Differentiation

Model how to complete the *Conflict-Resolution Map* activity sheet, and provide examples for English language learners. Encourage discussion first, and then allow them to work in pairs to complete the activity. They can also use pictures. Encourage above-level students to use higher-level thinking skills. Have them think of alternate solutions to the conflict. Use prompting and questioning with below-level students to help them identify the more complex conflicts and resolutions. Or provide the information for one side of the diagram and ask them to complete the other side.

Conflict-Resolution Map (cont.)

Grades 1–2 Example

Conflict(s)

Three baby owls are scared. They can't find their mother.

Resolution(s)

- The babies huddle together.
- Sarah tries to calm them down. She says why their mother might have left.
- The baby owls wait on a branch.
- The mother returns. The babies learned they don't need to be scared even if they are alone.

from *Owl Babies* by Martin Waddell

Grades 3–5 Example

Conflict(s)

Miss Nelson disappears and is replaced by a mean teacher, Miss Viola Swamp.

Resolution(s)

- The students from Room 207 talk to the police.
- They try to go to Miss Nelson's house to look for her, but they only see Miss Viola Swamp.
- When Miss Nelson returns, the students behave very well so that Miss Nelson will not disappear again.

from *Miss Nelson Is Missing!* by Harry Allard

Conflict-Resolution Map *(cont.)*

Grades 6–8 Example

Conflict(s)

- Boys are marooned on a deserted island with no adult supervision or guidance.

- They are torn between two human instincts: the desire to work to become a civilized society and the tendency to abandon themselves to savagery and chaos.

Resolution(s)

- Simon faces the Lord of the Flies in the jungle and realizes that the enemy and conflict is not external but rather inside each boy. When he tries to tell the other boys about his discovery, they kill him.

- As the other boys descend further into savagery, Ralph flees Jack's tribe to protect himself.

- Ralph encounters a naval officer on the beach, and the boys learn they will be rescued.

from *Lord of the Flies* by William Golding

Grades 9–12 Example

Conflict(s)

- The close relationship between Jim and Ántonia is strained when Jim goes to school to get an education, while Ántonia is forced to work to support her family.

- As an adult, Jim feels he will never be able to re-create the deep, loving friendship that he had with Ántonia.

Resolution(s)

- Jim spends time on Ántonia's farm and grows to admire and care for Ántonia's husband and children.

- He resolves to spend more time on the farm in order to get to know the Cuzak family better.

from *My Ántonia* by Willa Cather

Name: _____ **Date:** _____

Conflict-Resolution Map

Directions: Complete the graphic organizer by writing the conflict(s) and resolution(s).

Conflict(s)

What is the problem in the story?

What are the characters trying to resolve?

Resolution(s)

How is the problem overcome?

What are the effects of overcoming the conflict?

Semantic Word Map

Background Information

Semantic Word Maps (Heimlich and Pittelman 1986, as cited by Ryder and Graves 2003) allow students to clarify the meaning of concepts and identify connections to other related words by creating a map. This strategy is appropriate for studying a specific concept that has multiple vocabulary words. According to William Nagy and Judith Scott (2000), mapping the interconnectedness of vocabulary words is a way for students to organize and store information in the brain. Because this strategy builds a bridge between new information and previous knowledge and prior experiences, it also can be used as a preassessment to see what students already know about a given topic. Students can add to their Semantic Word Maps after they have completed the reading. Students also can use the maps to help them review information at the end of a unit of study or to write a paragraph or essay.

Grade Levels/Standards Addressed

See page 135 for the standards this strategy addresses, or refer to the Digital Resource CD (standards.pdf) to read the correlating standards in their entirety.

Stage of Writing Process

Prewrite

Activity

Determine the central concept of the assigned reading passage or lecture. After introducing the concept, lead a brainstorming session to create a list of words about it. Record all student ideas on the board, or use a document camera to display students' ideas. Distribute the *Semantic Word Map* activity sheet (page 152, semanticwordmap.pdf) to students. Encourage students to explain how these words relate to bigger ideas, events, characteristics, and examples, and help them move from the words to the concepts. Once the bigger categories have been determined, have students organize the words into categories. Students' maps should show big ideas, small ideas, and how all the ideas interconnect. Instruct students to share and explain their maps in small groups, making sure to justify and explain their reasons for choosing each word for each category.

Differentiation

Allow English language learners to work in small groups on this activity so that they can hear how other students determine categories and fit words into these categories. Encourage above-level students to incorporate additional or more complex words and categories, using resources to help them determine appropriate placement. Below-level students should work independently to generate a list of words and then work with a partner to determine the categories and the placement of the words. Working with partners provides students with support. Do not place these students in groups for this activity, as they will "fall through the cracks."

Semantic Word Map (cont.)

Grades 1–2 Example

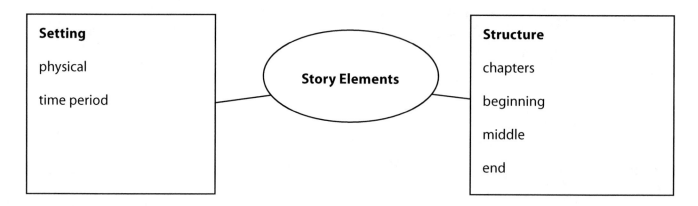

Setting

physical

time period

Story Elements

Structure

chapters

beginning

middle

end

Grades 3–5 Example

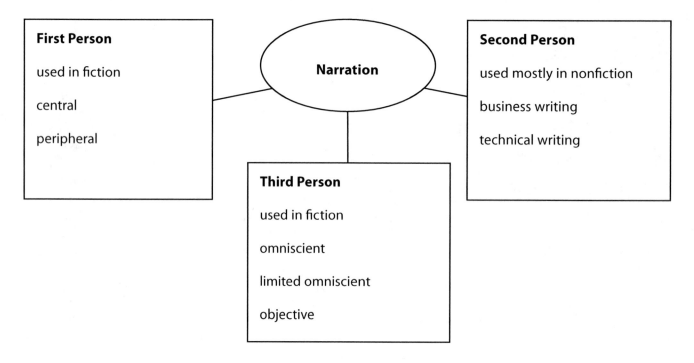

First Person

used in fiction

central

peripheral

Narration

Second Person

used mostly in nonfiction

business writing

technical writing

Third Person

used in fiction

omniscient

limited omniscient

objective

Semantic Word Map *(cont.)*

Grades 6–8 Example

Idiom

I'm in a pickle.

He was just in the nick of time.

Simile

He was as slow as a tortoise.

The rain poured down like juice from a pitcher.

Onomatopoeia

The faucet went *drip, drip* all through the night.

The owl hooted in the tree.

Figurative Language

Metaphor

She has a heart of gold.

You are my sunshine.

Personification

The sun greeted me as I opened the curtains.

Time creeps up on you.

Hyperbole

I will die if I have to be on stage.

His smile is a mile wide.

Grades 9–12 Example

Plot

backstory   poetic justice

foreshadowing   self-fulfilling
                  prophecy

cliffhanger
                  plot twist

flashback

Style

alliteration   onomatopoeia

symbolism   parody

imagery   satire

hyperbole   tone

Literary Techniques

Narrative Perspective

first person   unreliable
                 narrator

second person
                 omniscient

third person
                 magical realism

stream of
consciousness   epiphany

Character Development

personification

anthropomorphism

hamartia

pathetic fallacy

Semantic Word Map

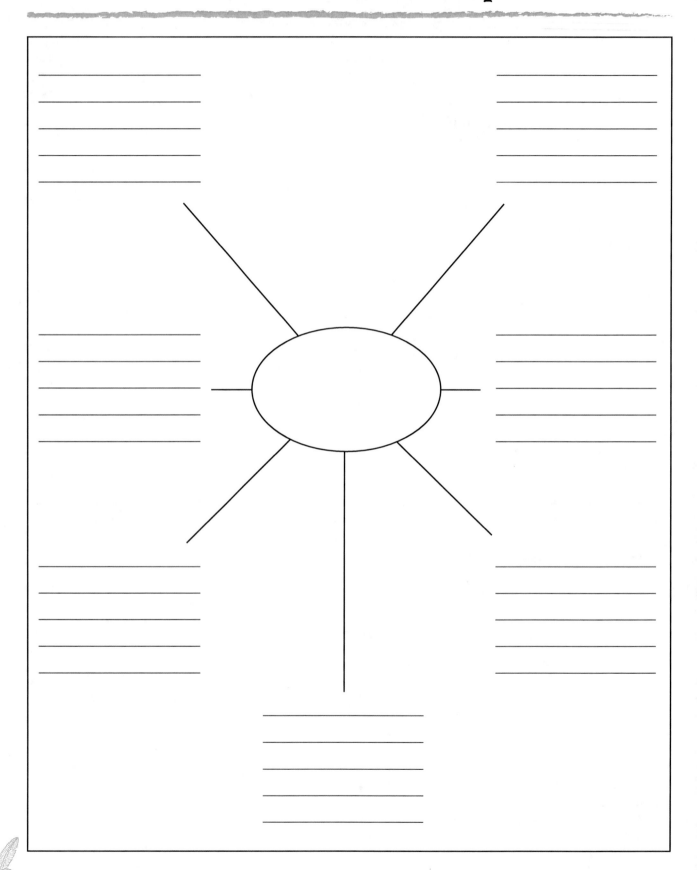

Story Strip

Background Information

By diagramming a story's plot sequence, students learn how to recall the series of events that occur during a story, summarize the main points, and analyze the text structure (Van Zile 2001). This strategy helps students create a visual and written representation of the plot, thereby increasing their comprehension of the story and providing students with a study tool for future reference. The Story Strip strategy can be used as a prewriting tool for organizing information gathered from a text selection or for developing ideas for future narrative writing assignments.

Grade Levels/Standards Addressed

See page 135 for the standards this strategy addresses, or refer to the Digital Resource CD (standards.pdf) to read the correlating standards in their entirety.

Stage of Writing Process

Prewrite

Activity

Before beginning the activity, review the concept of plot with students. Make sure to reinforce the idea that the plot is the sequence of events or actions that take place during a story. Advise students that they will be creating visual and written descriptions of the plot from an upcoming reading selection, so they should pay careful attention to the events that occur during the story. Read the story aloud, or have students read

it independently. Upon completion, hold a class discussion about the plot and help students recall the relevant events from the story. Note their ideas on the board or on a sheet of chart paper. Next, display the *Story Strip* activity sheet (page 156, storystrip.pdf) using a document camera, and demonstrate how to use the boxes to recreate events from the plot. Point out that the events need to be shown in chronological order and that only the most important events from the text selection should be included. Show students how to create a simple drawing of each event and write a description of the event underneath. Provide students with a list of transition words and phrases that they can use, such as *at the beginning, initially, next, then, at the end,* and *finally.*

Variation

This strategy can also be used as a prewriting activity to help students create their own fictional story lines. Prior to assigning a fictional writing task, demonstrate how students can use the Story Strip organizer to diagram the plot of the story they will be writing. Show them how to create drawings and jot down notes about the sequence of events that will occur over the duration of the story. Then explain how they can use the information on the Story Strip organizer as a guide when they actually begin to write the text of the story.

Differentiation

In this activity, below-level students will benefit from scaffolding. Give these students time to discuss the plot of the story with a partner and then have them draw the pictures independently. Assist them with writing some or all of the text as needed. Conduct a preview of the text with English language learners in order to familiarize them with the story content and new vocabulary words. If necessary, take dictation for the written portion of the Story Strip. Encourage above-level students to add details to both their drawings and their written descriptions. If these students finish early, have them create their own Story Strips based on ideas they have for stories they would like to write.

Story Strip (cont.)

Grades 1–2 Example

Text: *Harry the Dirty Dog* by Gene Zion

When Harry hears the bath water, he hides the scrub brush and runs away from home.	Harry plays in lots of different places and gets very, very dirty.	Harry goes home and his family doesn't recognize him because he is so dirty.
Harry does all his tricks to try and show his family that it is really him, but they do not understand.	Harry digs up the scrub brush and brings it to his family and jumps in the bathtub. The little girl and boy give Harry a bath.	When he is clean, his family realizes that it is Harry and everyone is very happy.

Story Strip *(cont.)*

Grades 3–5 Example

Text: *Stellaluna* by Janell Cannon

An owl attacks Stellaluna's mother, and Stellaluna falls through the air and lands in a bird's nest.	Stellaluna learns how to act like a bird.	Stellaluna, Pip, Flitter, and Flap learn to fly, and then Stellaluna gets separated from the other birds.
Stellaluna meets a group of bats and learns that she is a bat, not a bird. She is reunited with her mother.	Pip, Flitter, and Flap go to meet Stellaluna's family and get lost trying to fly in the dark. Stellaluna rescues them.	Stellaluna realizes that she is very different from Pip, Flitter, and Flap, but they can all still be friends.

Name: _____ Date: _____

Story Strip

Directions: Draw a picture in the box and write a description below for each main event from the story. Make sure to show the events in chronological order.

Text: _____

Name: _____ **Date:** _____

Plot Diagram

Directions: Label the plot diagram with the elements from the story.

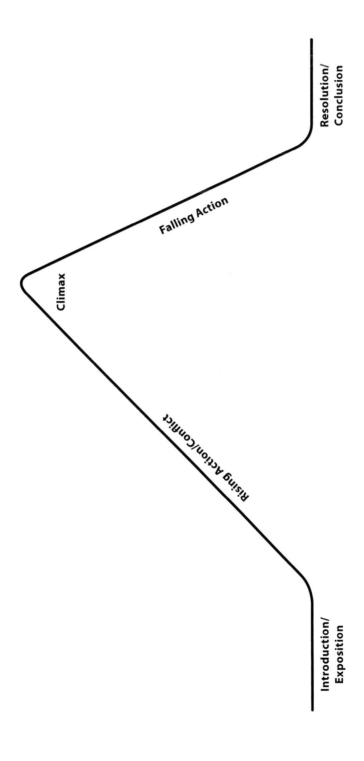

Text: _____

Climax

Falling Action

Resolution/Conclusion

Rising Action/Conflict

Introduction/Exposition

Authoring Overview

This book has previously established the strong connection between reading and writing. The quote from Gay Su Pinnell in the article "Success of Children at Risk in a Program That Combines Writing and Reading" bears repeating: "As children read and write they make the connections that form their basic understandings about both. Learning in one area enhances learning in the other. There is ample evidence to suggest that the processes are inseparable and that we should examine pedagogy in the light of these relationships. Hence, the two activities should be integrated in instructional settings. Teachers need to create supportive situations in which children have opportunities to explore the whole range of literacy learning, and they need to design instruction that helps children make connections between reading and writing" (1988).

Reading and writing are critical to all learning. Writing to apply new knowledge can be more challenging for students because they need to not only understand the content and be able to process it at a higher level but also communicate it using the strategies of the writing process, the features of the chosen genre, and the conventions of the grade level. Through authoring, students can make personal connections with the new content information they are learning.

Carol Santa, Lynn Havens, and Shirley Harrison (1996) make several key points regarding this connection.

1. **Writing helps students become more active learners.** Creating writing pieces that utilize content knowledge requires students to think more deeply about the content, analyze it, and reconstruct it into a piece of writing.

2. **Writing assists students in understanding the complexities of domain-specific material.** Writing can provide opportunities for students to analyze new concepts, internalize new vocabulary, and explore patterns and relationships between concepts.

3. **Writing forces learners to organize their thinking and to evaluate whether they have understood a concept.** In order to communicate in writing, students must carefully consider how to approach the writing activity. For example, students who are asked to write a narrative about a historical event must not only organize the content information that they intend to include but also meld it with the style appropriate for the genre. Within the framework of the genre, students must decide how best to communicate their information.

4. **One cannot write about something one does not understand.** The process of creating a clear explanation of a concept will challenge students to think carefully about the best way to explain it. In working through this challenge, students can develop a deeper understanding of the concept.

Authoring Overview *(cont.)*

Standards Addressed

The following chart shows the correlating standards for each strategy in this section. Refer to the Digital Resource CD (standards.pdf) to read the correlating standards in their entirety.

Strategy	McREL Standards	Common Core State Standards
Guided Writing Procedure	Grades 3–5 (1.1, 1.2) Grades 6–8 (1.1, 1.2) Grades 9–12 (1.1, 1.2)	Grade 3 (CCRA.W.9, W.3.2, W.3.5) Grade 4 (W.4.2, W.4.5, W.4.9) Grade 5 (W.5.2, W.5.5, W.5.9) Grade 6 (W.6.2, W.6.5, W.6.9) Grade 7 (W.7.2, W.7.5, W.7.9) Grade 8 (W.8.2, W.8.5, W.8.9) Grades 9–10 (W.9–10.2, W.9–10.5, W.9–10.9) Grades 11–12 (W.11–12.2, W.11–12.5, W.11–12.9)
Read, Encode, Annotate, Ponder	Grades 3–5 (1.4, 1.11) Grades 6–8 (1.4, 1.12) Grades 9–12 (1.4, 1.12)	Grade 3 (CCRA.W.9, W.3.8, SL.3.1) Grade 4 (W.4.8, W.4.9, SL.4.1) Grade 5 (W.5.8, W.5.9, SL.5.1) Grade 6 (W.6.8, W.6.9, SL.6.1) Grade 7 (W.7.8, W.7.9, SL.7.1) Grade 8 (W.8.8, W.8.9, SL.8.1) Grades 9–10 (W.9–10.8, W.9–10.9, SL.9–10.1) Grades 11–12 (W.11–12.8, W.11–12.9, SL.11–12.1)

Authoring Overview (cont.)

Strategy	McREL Standards	Common Core State Standards
Collaborative Writing	Grades 3–5 (1.1, 1.4) Grades 6–8 (1.1, 1.4) Grades 9–12 (1.1, 1.4)	Grade 3 (W.3.5, W.3.10, SL.3.1) Grade 4 (W.4.5, W.4.10, SL.4.1) Grade 5 (W.5.5, W.5.10, SL.5.1) Grade 6 (W.6.5, W.6.10, SL.6.1) Grade 7 (W.7.5, W.7.10, SL.7.1) Grade 8 (W.8.5, W.8.10, SL.8.1) Grades 9–10 (W.9–10.5, W.9–10.10, SL.9–10.1) Grades 11–12 (W.11–12.5, W.11–12.10, SL.11–12.1)
Author's Chair	Grades 1–2 (1.4) Grades 3–5 (1.4) Grades 6–8 (1.4) Grades 9–12 (1.4)	Grade 1 (W.1.5, SL.1.1) Grade 2 (W.2.5, SL.2.1) Grade 3 (W.3.5, SL.3.1) Grade 4 (W.4.5, SL.4.1) Grade 5 (W.5.5, SL.5.1) Grade 6 (W.6.5, SL.6.1) Grade 7 (W.7.5, SL.7.1) Grade 8 (W.8.5, SL.8.1) Grades 9–10 (W.9–10.5, SL.9–10.1) Grades 11–12 (W.11–12.5, SL.11–12.1)

Guided Writing Procedure

Background Information

The Guided Writing Procedure (Smith and Bean 1980) uses writing as a vehicle for activating students' prior knowledge and synthesizing existing and new information. Students brainstorm around a topic to lay a foundation for building new content knowledge and then analyze the information for patterns and relationships to create an outline, just as good writers do during the prewriting phase. After writing a paragraph, students compare their work with that of the language arts textbook, fictional passage, or trade book to look for similarities and differences and opportunities to add or change information.

Grade Levels/Standards Addressed

See page 163 for the standards this strategy addresses, or refer to the Digital Resource CD (standards.pdf) to read the correlating standards in their entirety.

Stages of Writing Process

Prewrite, Draft, Revise

Activity

Write the key concept for the lesson on the board. Ask students to brainstorm everything they know about that concept, and write their responses on the board. Remind them that there are no "wrong" ideas in brainstorming. Then, review the brainstormed ideas as a class, decide what the major points are and which are supporting details, and create a simple outline as a prewriting strategy. Provide time for students to draft a paragraph or two using the class outline. Next, have students read the assigned text and analyze their work against the provided text. They should see how well the class outline matches the language arts text, look for similarities and differences between their own paragraph(s) and the text, and identify information that could be added or deleted from their writing, based on the provided text.

Differentiation

Scaffold notes or create an outline for English language learners to use as they write their paragraphs. Model the strategy and provide examples of completed paragraphs for these students to refer to. Have above-level students write more than a paragraph on the topic. Conduct writing conferences with below-level students to explicitly instruct how to use notes from the prewriting stage to create a draft. Also, provide models of good paragraphs and spend time in the conferences analyzing the good writing traits shown in the examples. Use students' work to guide them through analyzing their writing and the text for similarities and differences. Understanding and being able to recognize good writing helps these students become better writers themselves.

Guided Writing Procedure (cont.)

Grades 3–5 Example

Concept: summarizing

Brainstorming:

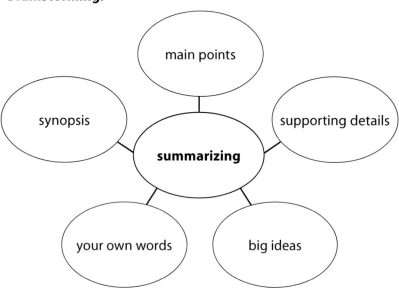

Sample Paragraph:

Summarizing is an important skill to learn because it helps you get an idea about the overall meaning of a text or lecture. When you summarize, you need to write down just the main points and supporting details, leaving out the minor details. You also need to write in your own words and not copy or quote directly from the text or speech. To write a summary of a fictional story, it is important to include the characters, the main events of the plot, the conflict, and the resolution.

Grades 6–8 Example

Concept: theme

Brainstorming:

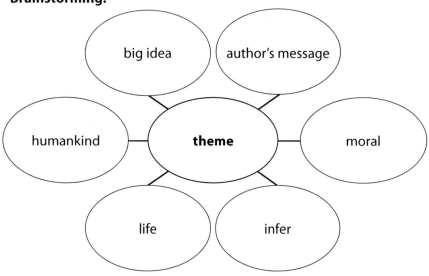

Sample Paragraph:

The theme is the underlying message the author wants to convey to the reader. In fables, the theme, or big idea, is often stated explicitly in the form of a moral at the end of the story. In most fiction, however, the reader must infer the theme as it is developed throughout the story. Themes often deal with important topics concerning life or humankind. Common themes include love, jealousy, perseverance, grief, and the power of family.

Guided Writing Procedure *(cont.)*

Grades 9–12 Example

Concept: literary analysis

Brainstorming:

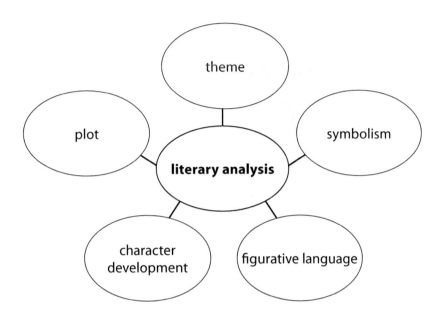

Sample Paragraph:

A literary analysis of a fictional narrative includes the examination of a variety of literary components that the story comprises. The writer may choose to focus on one element, such as character development, or complete an analysis of multiple literary devices. Literary analysis generally includes the study of theme, symbolism, figurative language, character development, and/or plot. Often, an analysis combines two or more elements; for example, one might examine how the author uses symbolism to develop the theme of the text. The objective of a literary analysis to gain a greater understanding of the text and the methods the author used to convey the central ideas in the literature.

Read, Encode, Annotate, Ponder

Background Information

The purpose of the Read, Encode, Annotate, Ponder (REAP) strategy (Eanet and Manzo 1976) is to help students develop a greater understanding of the author's role in writing and to improve their reading comprehension. REAP helps students build a bridge between the text and their own words to enable them to communicate their understanding of the text. This strategy facilitates the recall and summarization of information from narrative texts. Through this strategy, students learn to paraphrase texts and then reflect on this information in order to analyze how the author's point of view and attitude affect his or her writing.

Grade Levels/Standards Addressed

See page 163 for the standards this strategy addresses, or refer to the Digital Resource CD (standards.pdf) to read the correlating standards in their entirety.

Stage of Writing Process

Draft

Activity

Distribute the *Read, Encode, Annotate, Ponder* activity sheet (page 173, reap.pdf) prior to reading a selected fictional text. The steps represented by the acronym are as follows:

R—Read and understand the text. After students read the assigned story, have them discuss the contents of the text with partners, in small groups, or in a whole-class discussion.

E—Encode the author's words into their own words. Have students put in their own words what the text passage says. They should be able to do this without having to reread the material as they talk about it. They should become familiar enough with the text to discuss it comfortably. *What is the main idea? Who are the characters? What happens in the story?*

A—Annotate what they are reading. Annotation is not just a summary of what students have read. Instead, it is an extension of or elaboration on the text. Prompt students with these questions:

- What is the tone of the text? What does that tell you about the author's attitude?

- What is the conflict being presented in the story? How does it relate to the theme?

- Analyze the writing in the text. Is it clear? Could it be improved? Is it creative in how it is presented? Does it need any clarification or additions?

- What is the author's purpose or intention for writing?

- What can you learn from the author's writing that will help your own writing?

P—Pondering means that students must think about what they have written. Does it make sense? Does it complement or differ from what was said in the text?

Name: _____ **Date:** _____

Read, Encode, Annotate, Ponder

Study Topic/Reading Assignment: _____

R—Read and understand the author's ideas. Do you understand what you are reading? Do you understand all the words? Do you need help with understanding anything?
E—Encode the author's words into your own words. What is the author saying? What is the main idea or concept being presented? Who are the characters? What happens in the story? Explain it in your own words.
A—Annotate what you read. What is the tone of the text? What does it tell you about the author's point of view? What is the conflict presented in the text? How does it relate to the theme? What can you learn from the author's writing that will help your own?
P—Ponder what you have written. Does it make sense? Would someone else understand what you have written? Is it accurate? Do you need to change anything? Did you use your own words?

Collaborative Writing

Background Information

Writing is often thought of as an individual activity, but the Collaborative Writing strategy illustrates the benefits of working together with two or more people to create a written text. Collaborative Writing is an extension of the cooperative-learning pedagogy where students work in small groups to maximize their learning (Speck 2002). There are many different ways to format and structure collaborative writing projects, but all projects should provide each group member with the chance to participate in each phase of the writing process: brainstorming/prewriting, drafting, revising/editing, and publishing. Collaborative writing enables students to benefit from the direct guidance and support of their peers while also gaining routine writing experience and exposure to multiple writing styles.

Grade Levels/Standards Addressed

See page 164 for the standards this strategy addresses, or refer to the Digital Resource CD (standards.pdf) to read the correlating standards in their entirety.

Stages of Writing Process

Prewrite, Draft, Revise

Preparation

Structure

Before beginning the activity, decide on how to structure the Collaborative Writing activity. First, decide whether students will participate in sequential writing or parallel writing. For sequential writing, one student starts writing and then passes the document to the next student, who continues writing, and so forth. This structure works well with narrative writing in which students can easily build on what has already been written. Parallel writing occurs when the writing assignment is divided between the group members and all students work on their individual portions simultaneously. This format is more conducive to expository writing in which various sections can be identified by topic and worked on individually. Once all of the group members have completed their designated portions, they combine the sections and revise and edit to create a final product.

Topic

Another consideration with Collaborative Writing is the writing topic. The teacher should decide beforehand whether students will choose their own topics, the teacher will assign a universal topic for the entire class, or students will choose from a list or a specific, narrow focus area.

Groups

Lastly, it is important to decide how to group students. The teacher can assign students to particular groups, choosing to make either heterogeneous groups with multiple ability levels or homogeneous groups that are leveled by students' skills and capabilities. Alternatively, students can choose their own groups based on common interests or desired writing topics.

Collaborative Writing (cont.)

Activity

Begin the lesson by explaining the concept of collaborative writing. Describe how collaborative writing enables students to learn from one another and to pool their collective creativity to produce a finished product. Divide students into groups or help them divide themselves, and then explain how each student in the group will have a designated role and be expected to participate fully in the writing process. If students will be doing sequential writing, help them decide the order in which they will write. If students will be doing parallel writing, demonstrate how they can divide the writing assignment into separate portions based on topics or main points. Before they begin writing, provide students with time to work together on a prewriting activity. This activity may take the form of an outline, a concept map, a plot diagram, etc. The teacher should move from group to group, facilitating discussion and helping resolve any challenges that arise.

Once the prewriting activity is complete, invite students to begin writing independently, keeping the group plan in mind. The drafting portion of Collaborative Writing may be relatively short and completed within the time limits of a single class, or it may be much longer and completed over a period of days or weeks. After the initial drafting phase, groups reconvene to begin the process of revising and editing. This is often the most difficult portion of Collaborative Writing because of the challenges associated with uniting multiple authors under a common style and voice. Provide students with specific guidance on how to think about the revising process and suggestions for managing the task. Depending on the age and ability level, it may be easier for one student to revise and edit the document, incorporating his or her changes before handing it to the next student for review. On the other hand, some students may prefer to go through the document together as a group, reading portions aloud, discussing possible changes, and coming to a group consensus before making substantial revisions to the document.

When groups complete their writing projects, provide them with ample opportunities to share their work with other groups or audiences. Collaborative Writing is not only challenging from an academic perspective but also from a social standpoint, and students will benefit from multiple opportunities to reflect on their experiences throughout the process.

Differentiation

The Collaborative Writing strategy can be challenging for students of all ability levels, so careful consideration of individual strengths and weaknesses is necessary. English language learners should be grouped with patient students who are willing to provide them with assistance. The teacher should conference with English language learners individually before they begin writing in order to provide additional guidance or scaffolding for the writing task. If desired, above-level students can be encouraged to take on leadership roles in their groups and help other students where appropriate. Extra supervision may be necessary to ensure that these students do not completely take over the responsibilities of the other group members. Below-level students will benefit from extra guidance during the prewriting and drafting phases in order to build confidence and ensure comprehension of each stage of the writing process.

Author's Chair

Background Information

The Author's Chair strategy (Karelitz 1982; Boutwell 1983; Calkins 1983; Graves 1983; Graves and Hansen 1983) provides student writers with feedback on their writing. It has also been called *peer conferencing*. Researchers and educators continue to confirm the strong connections between reading and writing and between authors and readers. The focus of the Author's Chair strategy is to provide feedback to students on their writing: acknowledging its good qualities, making specific suggestions for improvement, and asking thought-provoking questions of the student authors. This strategy provides the guidance necessary for students to strengthen their writing through the integration of thoughts, suggestions, and criticisms provided by their peers and other adults in a supportive environment.

Grade Levels/Standards Addressed

See page 164 for the standards this strategy addresses, or refer to the Digital Resource CD (standards.pdf) to read the correlating standards in their entirety.

Stage of Writing Process

Revise

Activity

Ask students to select a writing piece, and place them in groups of no more than four. Give each group the following tasks:

- Students take turns reading their pieces of writing aloud.

- Group members listen intently and share their feedback.

- Once all members of the group have shared their writing and received feedback, instruct students to compare their work to other published texts. How does their writing compare with professional writers? What can be learned about writing from professional writers? What can be learned about how the authors structure and organize their writing?

- Allow time for students to edit and revise their writing. Students can use this time to incorporate into their writing suggestions from peers as well as ideas from professional writers. If time permits, allow small groups to meet again and repeat the strategy.

Variation

With primary grade students, conduct the strategy as a whole class. Choose one or two students to read their writing pieces to the class, and then ask the class to provide feedback. Remind students to offer specific comments.

Author's Chair *(cont.)*

Differentiation

Hold individual writing conferences with English language learners and below-level students to provide direct instruction and specific feedback. Consider using a lower-level text as a model so that the reading level does not hinder their abilities to analyze writing qualities. These students can join groups when it is time to peruse language arts materials and texts. Group above-level students with others who will challenge their writing skills. Ask them to share the techniques they learned from reviewing the professional writing and how they plan to incorporate these techniques into their own writing.

Grades 1–2 Example

Student Writing Sample:

Once upon a time, a mean old witch lived in a hidden cave. She slept all day. She only came out at night to scare little kids. One day, a small girl found the witch sleeping in her cave. She was not afraid at all. She walked into the cave and yelled, "Hello!" This scared the sleeping witch and she jumped. The witch learned that it was not fun to be scared like that. So she decided she would not scare little kids anymore. Then she was a nice witch.

Class Comments:

Student 1: I think it is good that you started with "Once upon a time" because the story reminds me of a fairy tale.

Student 2: I think you could find a more interesting word to describe the witch than mean. What about evil or mischievous?

Student 3: I think you should add a little more detail to the last sentence. How did she act as a nice witch?

Student 4: I like how it was a young girl that taught the witch the lesson.

Author's Chair (cont.)

Grades 3–5 Example
Student Writing Sample:

In the small town of Yuka, a little boy named Sam lived with his mother, father, and older sister. They lived in a little log cabin in the woods because they did not have very much money. Sam's mother, father, and sister worked hard all day planting vegetables, cutting trees for firewood, and hunting birds and squirrels. Sam did not like to work, though. He just liked to climb up into a tree and daydream about imaginary people and places.

Class Comments:

Student 1: I like the way you start your story by introducing the setting and characters.

Student 2: I think the second sentence needs clarification. Where would they rather live if they had more money? Some people choose to live in log cabins in the woods even if they do have lots of money.

Student 3: You did a good job setting up the conflict. I can tell that Sam's tendency to daydream and not helping with the work will be a big problem in the story. The way you structured the opening paragraph makes me want to keep reading and find out what happens next.

Grades 6–8 Example
Student Writing Sample:

The lights dimmed in the theater, and the movie flickered to life on the screen. I could smell the popcorn and hear the rustling of many people in the seats around me. A young girl giggled in the row behind me, and someone coughed quietly up in front. My friend Sarah sat beside me, contentedly popping candy into her mouth and humming along with the opening music. I had never felt so alone in my entire life.

Class Comments:

Student 1: You did a great job describing the setting for the opening of your story. I like all the details you included about the movie theater. Your description was very realistic.

Student 2: I loved your opening paragraph! The imagery you used to describe the movie theater was very realistic; I felt like I was actually sitting there with the narrator. I also like the irony of the last sentence. I definitely want to read the rest of your story!

Student 3: I like the way you started this paragraph, but I think you could add even more details and examples to make of the last sentence more sarcastic. Maybe you could mention something about the sense of touch, like the close proximity of the people around you.

GIST *(cont.)*

Grades 3–5 Example
Text: *Heidi* by Johanna Spyri

Passage

From the old and pleasantly situated village of Mayenfeld, a footpath winds through green and shady meadows to the foot of the mountains, which on this side look down from their stern and lofty heights upon the valley below. The land grows gradually wilder as the path ascends, and the climber has not gone far before he begins to inhale the fragrance of the short grass and sturdy mountain-plants, for the way is steep and leads directly up to the summits above.

On a clear sunny morning in June two figures might be seen climbing the narrow mountain path; one, a tall strong-looking girl, the other a child whom she was leading by the hand, and whose little cheeks were so aglow with heat that the crimson color could be seen even through the dark, sunburnt skin. And this was hardly to be wondered at, for in spite of the hot June sun the child was clothed as if to keep off the bitterest frost.

Key Points

setting
   foothills at the base of mountains
   June
   hot weather

characters
   older girl
   tall and strong-looking
   young girl
   dressed in numerous layers even
   though it is not cold

Summary (No more than 20 words)
An older girl is leading a young girl dressed in many layers up a path that leads to the mountains.

Grades 6–8 Example
Text: *Frankenstein* by Mary Shelley

Passage

But I have one want which I have never yet been able to satisfy, and the absence of the object of which I now feel as a most severe evil, I have no friend, Margaret: when I am glowing with the enthusiasm of success, there will be none to participate my joy; if I am assailed by disappointment, no one will endeavour to sustain me in dejection. I shall commit my thoughts to paper, it is true; but that is a poor medium for the communication of feeling. I desire the company of a man who could sympathize with me, whose eyes would reply to mine. You may deem me romantic, my dear sister, but I bitterly feel the want of a friend. I have no one near me, gentle yet courageous, possessed of a cultivated as well as of a capacious mind, whose tastes are like my own, to approve or amend my plans. How would such a friend repair the faults of your poor brother!

Key Points

loneliness
   lack of friend
   no one with whom to share joy or ease
   disappointment
   nothing can take the place of human
   friendship
   friendship helps overcome individual
   personal faults

Summary (No more than 20 words)
The narrator is lonely and wants a friend with whom he can share his joys, disappointments, and personal shortcomings.

GIST (cont.)

Grades 9–12 Example

Text: *Pride and Prejudice* by Jane Austen

Passage

It is a truth universally acknowledged, that a single man in possession of a good fortune, must be in want of a wife.

However little known the feelings or views of such a man may be on his first entering a neighbourhood, this truth is so well fixed in the minds of the surrounding families, that he is considered the rightful property of some one or other of their daughters.

Key Points

single man
    good fortune
    assumed to want a wife
    moves into a new neighborhood
    surrounding families consider him
    property to be married to one of their
    daughters

Summary (No more than 20 words)

When a single man with money moves into a neighborhood, the neighbors assume he will marry one of their daughters.

Name: _____ **Date:** _____

GIST

Directions: After reading the text, write down the key points and write a summary of no more than 20 words.

Key Points

_____   _____   _____

_____   _____   _____

_____   _____   _____

_____   _____   _____

_____   _____   _____

Summary

_____

_____

_____

_____

_____

_____

_____

_____

_____

Key Words

Background Information

Key Words (Hoyt 1999) is a summary strategy that is better suited to younger students because it does not limit the number of words used in a summary. It provides greater scaffolding to support students in creating a clear, concise summary. Before summarizing, students are asked to simply identify the key words from the text. Those words are then used to compose the summary. Key Words can also be effective for older students who are learning to write summaries in multiparagraph compositions.

Grade Levels/Standards Addressed

See page 181 for the standards this strategy addresses, or refer to the Digital Resource CD (standards.pdf) to read the correlating standards in their entirety.

Stages of Writing Process

Prewrite, Draft, Revise

Activity

Explain that students are to look for the main ideas, or key words, as they read a selected fictional text. Distribute scrap paper, sticky notes, or notebook paper to students on which to write the key words. After the reading, call on students to share their words, discuss the significance of each one, and justify their choices to develop a class list of the key words from the text. Model and discuss how to organize, rearrange, and delete duplicate key words as needed. Then, write a summary using the key words, either by modeling the entire process or using the Guided Writing Procedure strategy (see pages 165–167). Model for students how to edit and revise the summary so it flows naturally. Provide students with adequate guided-practice time before allowing them to write a summary independently, and make sure to highlight the importance of using their own words rather than copying phrases straight from the text.

Differentiation

Preview the text, and preteach any new vocabulary words for English language learners to improve their comprehension. Guide these students in a small group to develop their summaries. Give above-level students reading materials that are appropriate for their reading level, and challenge them by limiting the number of words used in their summaries. Scaffold for below-level students by modeling how to identify key words as they read.

Key Words (cont.)

Grades 1–2 Example

Text Passage:

As the weather turned colder and the leaves fell from the trees, the great bear began to search for a place to hibernate for the winter.

Key Words:

bear, hibernate, winter

Summary:

The bear was looking for a place to hibernate during the winter.

Grades 3–5 Example

Text Passage:

His mean words echoed in my head and my vision blurred with tears at the memory of his cruel taunts. How could I have ever thought he was a true friend?

Key Words:

mean words, cruel taunts, true friend

Summary:

The boy's mean words and cruel taunts made it clear he was not a true friend.

Guided Reading and Summarizing Procedure

Background Information

The Guided Reading and Summarizing Procedure (Hayes 1989, as cited by Ryder and Graves 2003; Lenski, Wham, and Johns 1999) teaches students to summarize independently. Students learn to gather, recall, organize, and self-correct information before composing a summary through teacher modeling. Ryder and Graves (2003) suggest that students and the teacher subsequently write summaries individually, and then compare and contrast students' summaries to that of the teacher. According to Ryder and Graves (2003), research suggests the teacher revise his or her summary based on students' suggestions and make a visible record of these changes. This process will demonstrate how students can develop and strengthen their own writing by planning, revising, and editing effectively.

Grade Levels/Standards Addressed

See page 181 for the standards this strategy addresses, or refer to the Digital Resource CD (standards.pdf) to read the correlating standards in their entirety.

Stages of Writing Process

Prewrite, Draft, Revise

Activity

Explain to students that they will use the Guided Reading and Summarizing Procedure to help them summarize the information in a text. Emphasize the importance of learning how to summarize text and knowing when summarizing is needed. When students have finished reading the selected fictional text, have them share what they remember. Write their comments on the board or display them with a document camera. Then, have students read the text again, this time looking for any information they missed that can be elaborated on, or that is inaccurate. Make changes as needed and then organize the ideas into main ideas and details. Using this class outline, model how to write a summary passage for students. Read through the summary as a class to edit and revise it, demonstrating how to make changes so that it flows naturally and contains all the important points from the text passage. After learning how to use the strategy, students can use the *Guided Reading and Summarizing Procedure* activity sheet (page 192, grasp.pdf) to write their summaries independently.

Differentiation

Remind English language learners and below-level students to use the text as reference. English language learners might also benefit from having a sheet with the key points to use in their summary statements. Above-level students can complete this activity independently from the beginning.

Character Summary *(cont.)*

Grades 3–5 Example

Text: *Chocolate Fever* by Robert Kimmel Smith

Character: Henry Green

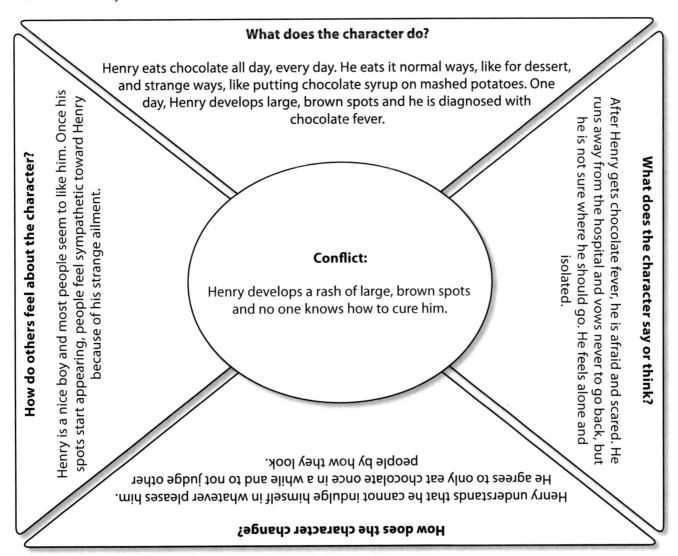

What does the character do?

Henry eats chocolate all day, every day. He eats it normal ways, like for dessert, and strange ways, like putting chocolate syrup on mashed potatoes. One day, Henry develops large, brown spots and he is diagnosed with chocolate fever.

How do others feel about the character?

Henry is a nice boy and most people seem to like him. Once his spots start appearing, people feel sympathetic toward Henry because of his strange ailment.

What does the character say or think?

After Henry gets chocolate fever, he is afraid and scared. He runs away from the hospital and vows never to go back, but he is not sure where he should go. He feels alone and isolated.

Conflict:

Henry develops a rash of large, brown spots and no one knows how to cure him.

How does the character change?

Henry understands that he cannot indulge himself in whatever pleases him. He agrees to only eat chocolate once in a while and to not judge other people by how they look.

Author's theme or point of view:

The theme of this book is that we cannot have everything we want every time we want it, and that it is possible to have too much of a good thing.

Character Summary (cont.)

Grades 6–8 Example

Text: *Little Women* by Louisa May Alcott

Character: Jo March

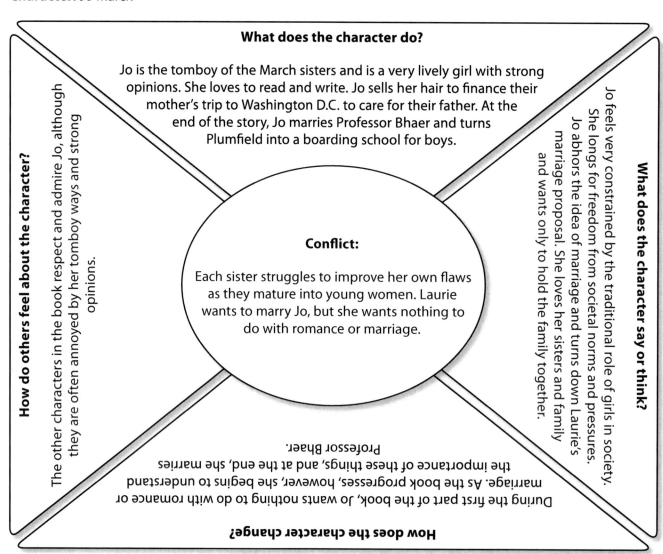

What does the character do?

Jo is the tomboy of the March sisters and is a very lively girl with strong opinions. She loves to read and write. Jo sells her hair to finance their mother's trip to Washington D.C. to care for their father. At the end of the story, Jo marries Professor Bhaer and turns Plumfield into a boarding school for boys.

How do others feel about the character?

The other characters in the book respect and admire Jo, although they are often annoyed by her tomboy ways and strong opinions.

Conflict:

Each sister struggles to improve her own flaws as they mature into young women. Laurie wants to marry Jo, but she wants nothing to do with romance or marriage.

What does the character say or think?

Jo feels very constrained by the traditional role of girls in society. She longs for freedom from societal norms and pressures. Jo abhors the idea of marriage and turns down Laurie's marriage proposal. She loves her sisters and family and wants only to hold the family together.

How does the character change?

During the first part of the book, Jo wants nothing to do with romance or marriage. As the book progresses, however, she begins to understand the importance of these things, and at the end, she marries Professor Bhaer.

Author's theme or point of view:

The author showcases the struggle of balancing personal growth with familial duty through all the sisters but especially through Jo's development over the course of the story.

Story Mapping *(cont.)*

Grades 9–12 Example

Text: *Johnny Tremain* by Esther Forbes Hoskins

Characters

Johnny Tremain, Rab Silsbee, Priscilla (Cilla) Lapham, Ephraim Lapham, Lavinia Lyte Tremain, Isannah Lapham, Dove, Dusty, John Hancock, Jonathan Lyte, Mr. Lorne, Mrs. Lorne

Setting

1773–1775—years preceding the Revolutionary War

Colonial Boston

Describe the Problem(s)

The American colonists struggle to gain independence from the British.

Johnny fights to overcome his arrogant and selfish ways so he can become a better man.

Event 1

Johnny's hand is severely disfigured due to a prank by Dove. He has to find a new profession and place to live.

Event 2

Johnny becomes a spy for the rebellion and participates in the Boston Tea Party.

Event 3

The war begins between the colonists and the British. Johnny breaks completely with his past self and later learns that his disfigured hand can be fixed.

Describe the Solution

Through the humbling experience of learning to live with a disfigured hand, Rab's death, and his continued struggle for human rights, Johnny is able to leave his arrogant traits in the past and mature into a responsible and moral young man.

Name: _____ **Date:** _____

Story Mapping

Directions: Use the diagram below to create a map of the story.

Text: _____

Characters	Setting

Describe the problem(s)

Event 1

Event 2

Event 3

Describe the Solution

#51006—*Writing Strategies for Fiction* © *Shell Education*

Applying Knowledge Overview

What Does the Research Say?

Expressive writing and informative, or transactional, writing both play important roles in the language arts classroom. While expressive writing allows students to express themselves creatively, informative writing enables students to communicate information accurately and explain research through writing. Both types of writing require adequate instruction and practice in order to prove useful to students.

Most types of writing used to apply knowledge fall under the category of transactional writing. Transactional writing, as Britton et al. (1975) call it, is the kind of writing that has a specific purpose. There is the intent to produce or explain something. There is a specific audience, and the writer is responsible for what he or she says. Most transactional writing ends up as a finished product and is often called *product writing*. There is emphasis on what the final product will look like. This type of writing is more formal and is the type of writing often required for exams, business-related writing, and analytical essays. Examples of transactional writing in the language arts classroom include research reports, test questions, literary-analysis essays, and homework assignments.

Students should be taught how to produce informative writing and be provided with models and examples to follow. Teachers should be expected to teach students how to write formal essays and complete literature-based research assignments. With transactional writing, students are accountable for spelling, grammar, and punctuation decisions. Writing mechanics and organization are as much a part of the grade as the content will be.

One of the best ways for students to learn how to comprehend fictional texts is by analyzing narratives and extrapolating this knowledge to their own writing. Writing-to-apply activities provide students with the opportunity to write about literary concepts using established formats such as research assignments and essays. Writing for an audience requires understanding of subject, organization, and complex cognitive thought. Writing-to-apply activities encourage critical thinking skills in formal settings. These same skills can transfer to writing that will be done throughout life in the workplace and elsewhere.

Students can also apply their knowledge of fictional literature by producing their own narratives or fictional texts. While the strategies in this book do not strive to teach students how to write fiction, there are several strategies that encourage narrative writing as a means of demonstrating knowledge of character development or text structure.

The more students write, the more familiar and the more comfortable they will become with expressing their thoughts through writing. Students need instruction, direction, experience, and motivation to write. Using transactional or informative writing in the language arts classroom allows students to express their knowledge of language arts topics while developing and strengthening their writing skills. It also allows students to weave together the language of literature into everyday language and conversation. Finally, the routine use of writing as a tool to apply knowledge in the classroom increases students' abilities to write for a range of different tasks, purposes, and audiences.

Applying Knowledge Overview (cont.)

Standards Addressed

The following chart shows the correlating standards for each strategy in this section. Refer to the Digital Resource CD (standards.pdf) to read the correlating standards in their entirety.

Strategy	McREL Standards	Common Core State Standards
Summary-Writing Microtheme	Grades 3–5 (1.11) Grades 6–8 (1.12) Grades 9–12 (1.12)	Grade 3 (W.3.8) Grade 4 (W.4.8) Grade 5 (W.5.8) Grade 6 (W.6.8) Grade 7 (W.7.8) Grade 8 (W.8.8) Grades 9–10 (W.9–10.8) Grades 11–12 (W.11–12.8)
RAFT Assignment	Grades 1–2 (1.7, 1.8) Grades 3–5 (1.5, 1.6) Grades 6–8 (1.5) Grades 9–12 (1.5, 1.6)	Grade 1 (CCRA.W.4) Grade 2 (CCRA.W.4) Grade 3 (W.3.4) Grade 4 (W.4.4) Grade 5 (W.5.4) Grade 6 (W.6.4) Grade 7 (W.7.4) Grade 8 (W.8.4) Grades 9–10 (W.9–10.4) Grades 11–12 (W.11–12.4)
Formal Letter	Grades 1–2 (1.7) Grades 3–5 (1.12) Grades 6–8 (1.13) Grades 9–12 (1.13)	Grade 1 (CCRA.W.4) Grade 2 (CCRA.W.4) Grade 3 (W.3.4) Grade 4 (W.4.4) Grade 5 (W.5.4) Grade 6 (W.6.4) Grade 7 (W.7.4) Grade 8 (W.8.4) Grades 9–10 (W.9–10.4) Grades 11–12 (W.11–12.4)
Friendly Letter	Grades 1–2 (1.7) Grades 3–5 (1.12) Grades 6–8 (1.13) Grades 9–12 (1.13)	Grade 1 (CCRA.W.4) Grade 2 (CCRA.W.4) Grade 3 (W.3.4) Grade 4 (W.4.4) Grade 5 (W.5.4) Grade 6 (W.6.4) Grade 7 (W.7.4) Grade 8 (W.8.4) Grades 9–10 (W.9–10.4) Grades 11–12 (W.11–12.4)

Applying Knowledge Overview *(cont.)*

Strategy	McREL Standards	Common Core State Standards
Newspaper Article	Grades 1–2 (1.7) Grades 3–5 (1.7) Grades 6–8 (1.6) Grades 11–12 (1.7)	Grade 1 (CCRA.W.4) Grade 2 (CCRA.W.4) Grade 3 (W.3.4) Grade 4 (W.4.4) Grade 5 (W.5.4) Grade 6 (W.6.4) Grade 7 (W.7.4) Grade 8 (W.8.4) Grades 9–10 (W.9–10.4) Grades 11–12 (W.11–12.4)
Historical/Science Fiction Story	Grades 1–2 (1.7) Grades 3–5 (1.8) Grades 6–8 (1.7) Grades 9–12 (1.8)	Grade 1 (W.1.3) Grade 2 (W.2.3) Grade 3 (W.3.3) Grade 4 (W.4.3) Grade 5 (W.5.3) Grade 6 (W.6.3) Grade 7 (W.7.3) Grade 8 (W.8.3) Grades 9–10 (W.9–10.3) Grades 11–12 (W.11–12.3)
Character Diary	Grades 1–2 (1.7) Grades 3–5 (1.8) Grades 6–8 (1.7) Grades 9–12 (1.8)	Grade 1 (CCRA.W.9, W.1.3) Grade 2 (CCRA.W.9, W.2.3) Grade 3 (CCRA.W.9, W.3.3) Grade 4 (W.4.3, W.4.9) Grade 5 (W.5.3, W.5.9) Grade 6 (W.6.3, W.6.9) Grade 7 (W.7.3, W.7.9) Grade 8 (W.8.3, W.8.9) Grades 9–10 (W.9–10.3, W.9–10.9) Grades 11–12 (W.11–12.3, W.11–12.9)
Story Additions	Grades 3–5 (1.8) Grades 6–8 (1.7) Grades 9–12 (1.8)	Grade 3 (CCRA.W.9, W.3.3, W.3.4) Grade 4 (W.4.3, W.4.4, W.4.9) Grade 5 (W.5.3, W.5.4, W.5.9) Grade 6 (W.6.3, W.6.4, W.6.9) Grade 7 (W.7.3, W.7.4, W.7.9) Grade 8 (W.8.3, W.8.4, W.8.9) Grades 9–10 (W.9–10.3, W.9–10.4, W.9–10.9) Grades 11–12 (W.11–12.3, W.11–12.4, W.11–12.9)

Summary-Writing Microtheme

Background Information

The Microthemes strategy, introduced by John C. Bean (1996), enables students to write what they know about a specific theme. In essence, the microtheme is a condensed version of a research report or essay, written on one side of a 5" x 8" index card. This strategy reveals what students do or do not know about a specific literary subject. It provides an opportunity for students to write informally using clear and accurate information for an intended audience. With this microtheme, students determine which details to eliminate and which to condense. Ideally, this application activity would follow practice with GIST, Key Words, or Guided Reading and Summarizing Procedures so that students are well prepared to create their own summaries independently. The focus of the Summary-Writing Microtheme is to improve students' comprehension and summarizing abilities.

Grade Levels/Standards Addressed

See page 206 for the standards this strategy addresses, or refer to the Digital Resource CD (standards.pdf) to read the correlating standards in their entirety.

Stages of Writing Process

Prewrite, Draft, Revise, Edit, Publish

Activity

Select a piece of text that is well suited for summary writing. Tell students that they will write a short summary about the text. Display a sample Summary-Writing Microtheme on the board or with a document camera, and discuss the organization (main ideas and details), tone (direct), language (content vocabulary), and other features (transition words). Set clear expectations for students so they will be successful. Next, model writing a Summary-Writing Microtheme using a prewriting strategy, drafting, revising, editing, and publishing. This is probably best done over several days or class periods. Distribute the *Summary-Writing Microtheme* activity sheet (page 209, summarywriting.pdf) to get students started on the writing process.

Differentiation

If appropriate, allow English language learners to use pictures or other visual representations in their microthemes. Remind these students to focus on summarizing the text in an organized manner. Consider providing them with summary frames or sentence stems if these will help English language learners better communicate the information. Do not hold English language learners accountable for spelling and writing conventions as much as for content. Have above-level students write a Summary-Writing Microtheme on two different texts about the same topic and then compare and contrast the information. Provide small-group instruction for below-level students at each stage of the writing process. These students may need support to organize their information in a systematic manner and to use the prewriting work to create a draft. Allow additional time for these students to accomplish the assignment.

Summary-Writing Microtheme

Directions: Use this prewriting planner to organize your Summary-Writing Microtheme.

Main Idea

_____

_____

Detail

_____

_____

Detail

_____

_____

Detail

_____

_____

Closing Statement

_____

_____

Reminders:

- Refer to the text to identify the main idea.
- Make sure the details support or are related to the main idea.
- Use this outline to write your draft.
- Add transition words (*most importantly*, *for example*, etc.).

RAFT Assignment

Background Information

RAFT stands for Role, Audience, Format, and Topic, the key ingredients of writing assignments (Santa, Havens, and Harrison 1996). This particular writing assignment alters the usual assignment in which students write a formal essay or report. With this activity, teachers can encourage creative application of language arts content knowledge. For example, after reading a fictional text selection, writers may be asked to write from the point of view of a specific character (role) speaking to the third-person narrator (audience) in a dialogue (format) about the possible alternative resolutions to the conflict presented in the story (topic).

Grade Levels/Standards Addressed

See page 206 for the standards this strategy addresses, or refer to the Digital Resource CD (standards.pdf) to read the correlating standards in their entirety.

Stages of Writing Process

Prewrite, Draft, Edit, Revise, Publish

Activity

Prepare the *RAFT Assignment* activity sheet (page 211, raft.pdf) by filling in the RAFT components. Distribute the *RAFT Assignment* activity sheet to students, and then hold a brainstorming session to share ideas on how to address each area in the writing. Provide plenty of time for students to collaborate and get excited about the assignment. Model writing your own RAFT Assignment, showing each step of the writing process before asking students to work on their own. If needed, provide students with copies of a genre-specific graphic organizer (see pages 133–161) during the prewriting phase.

Variation

Primary-grade teachers may want to create a RAFT Assignment as a whole class, using the shared writing process on a large sheet of chart paper. Provide a beginning for the writing piece, and then ask students to contribute ideas to continue the story. Invite various students to come up and write each sentence on the chart until the story is complete. If grade-level teams are working on the RAFT Assignment, teachers may rotate the completed stories so that students can see the creative ideas of the other classes.

Differentiation

Allow English language learners to draw pictures in a story map to get them started. Modify the writing expectations to meet their individual levels. Below-level students may need more explicit instruction in the chosen genre, so consider meeting with these students in small groups to preteach the features of the genre before beginning writing. Also, provide graphic organizers to help them stay organized. Above-level students may be thrilled with the freedom of the assignment. They should be able to work independently, but challenge them appropriately to develop their writing skills further.

RAFT Assignment

Directions: Use this prewriting planner to organize your RAFT Assignment.

Role: _____

Audience: _____

Form: _____

Topic: _____

Reminders:

- Think carefully about your role and your point of view.

- Consider how to best communicate to your audience.

- Use the traits of the writing form. You may wish to create a graphic organizer specific to that genre, such as a letter, a poem, an explanation, or a story.

- Stay focused on your topic.

Formal Letter

Background Information

Writing a formal letter is another expressive writing strategy that provides students with the opportunity to communicate with other people or obtain new information. If possible, send the formal letters out, and read and post replies as they come into the classroom.

Grade Levels/Standards Addressed

See page 206 for the standards this strategy addresses, or refer to the Digital Resource CD (standards.pdf) to read the correlating standards in their entirety.

Stages of Writing Process

Prewrite, Draft, Revise, Edit, Publish

Activity

Review the following questions with students:

- What is the purpose of a formal letter?
- Can you think of an example of a formal letter that contains a literary topic?
- What key features of a formal letter should be included?
- What are some tips for writing a formal letter relating to a literary topic?

Divide the class into groups of three or four. Have each group make a list of ideas for formal letters with a literary theme.

Examples may include the following:

- Write a letter to an author. Ask the author questions about his or her work of fiction.
- Write a letter to the editor of a newspaper that contains book reviews. Have students provide their opinions about a recently reviewed book.
- Write a letter to a publishing company asking about the publishing process.
- Write a letter to a library. Ask the reference librarian for book recommendations, ideas about literary themes or concepts, or book club ideas.

Allow time for students to share their responses with the class. Call on students to share examples of formal letters with a literary theme. Distribute the *Formal Letter* activity sheet (page 213, formalletter.pdf), and allow students to write a formal letter on a literary topic.

Differentiation

Encourage English language learners to write the letter independently, and pair them with a partner for editing and revising. Pair them with students who are comfortable with writing formally. Encourage above-level students to write letters on a controversial literary topic or book. This will require students to present a topic and think through the arguments to convince the reader of their opinions. Below-level students will benefit from working with a partner to write the letter.

Formal Letter

_____

_____

_____

_____

_____

_____

_____

To Whom It May Concern: (or) Dear _____,

_____

_____

_____

_____

_____

_____

_____

_____

_____

_____

_____,

_____

Friendly Letter

Background Information

Writing a friendly letter is another expressive writing strategy that provides students with the opportunity to communicate their ideas about a literary topic or piece of fictional literature. Send friendly letters out and read and post replies as they arrive.

Grade Levels/Standards Addressed

See page 206 for the standards this strategy addresses, or refer to the Digital Resource CD (standards.pdf) to read the correlating standards in their entirety.

Stages of Writing Process

Prewrite, Draft, Revise, Edit, Publish

Activity

Review the following questions with students:

- What is the purpose of a friendly letter?
- Can you think of an example of a friendly letter that contains a language arts topic?
- What key features of a friendly letter should be included?
- What are some tips for writing a friendly letter relating to a literary topic?

Divide the class into groups of three or four. Have each group make a list of examples of a friendly letter with a language arts theme. Examples may include the following:

- letter to a friend comparing and contrasting two pieces of fictional literature
- letter to a family member explaining what has been learned in language arts class
- letter to a friend encouraging him or her to read a particular piece of literature

Allow time for students to share their responses with the class. Call on students to share examples of friendly letters with a literary theme. Distribute the *Friendly Letter* activity sheet (page 215, friendlyletter.pdf), and allow students to write a friendly letter of their own on a literary topic.

Differentiation

Encourage English language learners to write letters independently, and pair them with partners for editing and revising. Pair them with students who are comfortable with writing friendly letters. Encourage above-level students to write about a more complex topic, or challenge them to include more advanced vocabulary and complex sentence structures. Below-level students will benefit from working with a partner to write the letter.

Friendly Letter

_____

Dear _____,

_____

_____

_____

_____

_____

_____

_____

_____

_____

_____

_____

_____,

_____

Newspaper Article

Background Information

Writing a newspaper article on a literature-based theme is another way for students to use literary concepts in everyday life. The article usually answers the *who, what, where, when, why,* and *how* questions.

Grade Levels/Standards Addressed

See page 207 for the standards this strategy addresses, or refer to the Digital Resource CD (standards.pdf) to read the correlating standards in their entirety.

Stages of Writing Process

Prewrite, Draft, Revise, Edit, Publish

Activity

Divide the class into groups of three or four and give each group a newspaper or an age-appropriate periodical to read as a model. Ask the groups to locate and cut out an article about a literary topic or a book review. Write the following list on the board, and discuss the elements of a newspaper article.

A newspaper article has:

- headline—This is a short, concise phrase that explains the main point of the article.

- byline—This is the name of the person who wrote the newspaper article.

- dateline—This lists the month, day, and year the article was written.

- illustration—An illustration is optional for a newspaper article. It can help bring the point of the story home to the reader.

- paragraph 1—This should answer the who, what, when, and where questions.

- paragraph 2—This should answer the how and why questions. Answering how and why takes the reader to the next step.

- final paragraph—This is usually a conclusion, summary, or list of future prospects.

Explain that a newspaper article addresses the five *W*s—*who, what, where, when,* and *why*—and anticipates and answers readers' questions. A newspaper article can address issues and questions related to literature, or it can review a particular text. Have students identify a literature-based topic about which they would like to write a newspaper article or book review. Distribute the *Newspaper Article* activity sheet (page 217, newspaperarticle.pdf) to students to help them analyze the model article plan for writing their own. Then, have them write their articles or book reviews on separate sheets of paper, being mindful to include some of the text features they observed in the model newspaper article. Students should work with their groups to provide feedback to one another and develop and strengthen their writing.

Differentiation

Make sure English language learners clearly understand the literary topic before beginning to write. Then, provide resource books for them to use during the writing process so that they can look up words. Take extra time to make sure all of the words and phrases on the board are clearly defined and understood by below-level students. Use visuals whenever possible. Both English language learners and below-level students will benefit from working in mixed-ability groups. Have above-level students work in teams to design a newspaper dedicated to the literary topics being studied in class.

Newspaper Article

Directions: Answer the questions below as they relate to your topic. Then, write your newspaper article on a separate sheet of paper, making sure to include some of the text features you marked in the original newspaper article.

Topic: _____

Who?

Who is the article about? _____

Who would be interested in reading it? _____

Who is the audience? _____

What?

What is the purpose of the article? _____

What is the main idea of the article? How does it relate to literature? _____

What is the author's desired result? _____

When?

When does the event in the story take place? _____

When was the story written? _____

Where?

Where does the news story take place? _____

Where is the newspaper circulated? _____

Why?

Why was this printed in the newspaper instead of a book or another reference? _____

Why did the events in the news story happen? _____

Why did the author write the article? What can be learned about literature as a result of this article? _____
_____

Historical/Science Fiction Story

Background Information

Writing a Historical/Science Fiction Story is a great way for students to weave content-area knowledge into everyday life. In order for a piece of fiction to be believable, it must contain convincing information on domain-specific topics. Look for opportunities throughout content-area lessons to point out science or social studies problems that could be turned into a story.

Grade Levels/Standards Addressed

See page 207 for the standards this strategy addresses, or refer to the Digital Resource CD (standards.pdf) to read the correlating standards in their entirety.

Stages of Writing Process

Prewrite, Draft, Revise, Edit, Publish

Activity

Read a chapter of a science fiction or historical fiction story. Identify with the class the domain-specific problem and possible solutions. Discuss the main elements of a story:

- setting
- characters
- problem
- solution

Explain that a story has a beginning, a middle, and an end. The beginning usually describes the setting and introduces the characters. The reader learns more about the characters and the problem in the middle of the story. The ending tells the solution to the problem. Point out that content-area facts and details need to be woven into the story and the plot. Work together as a class to write a story outline. Record student ideas on the board or display them with a document camera.

First, discuss the characters. Which characters should be in the story? Remember to limit the number of characters because too many characters can lead to confusion. Brainstorm with students some settings and problems for their stories. Spend time researching the content-area topic so students have a clear understanding of the topic and how it could be an issue in everyday life. Write each sentence as a class. Call on one student at a time to add to the story.

Once the story is written, read it to the class. Analyze how well the content-area elements were handled. Identify any changes or additions that need to be made. Then, have students use the *Historical/Science Fiction Story* activity sheet (page 219, historicalscience.pdf) to help plan and write their own fictional story.

Differentiation

Give English language learners resources such as dual-language dictionaries, picture books, and encyclopedias at their reading level. Hold frequent conferences with English language learners and below-level students throughout the writing process to provide modeling, feedback, and scaffolding. Challenge above-level students to include richer vocabulary, more dynamic language, and more complex sentence structures.

Historical/Science Fiction Story

Directions: Use this story map to help you plan your fictional story. Follow the arrows to the next step. Then, write your story on a separate sheet of paper.

Setting (Where and when does the story take place?)

Characters (Who or what are the people, animals, or objects in the story?)

Conflict/Problem (What is the content-area problem?)

Action/Events (What are the attempts to solve the problem?)

Solution (How does the story end?)

Character Diary

Background Information

The Character Diary strategy provides students with the opportunity to apply their knowledge about character development and plot to narrative writing. By writing diary entries from the perspective of a fictional character, students learn how to adopt the character's point of view, language style, opinions, and attitudes. This activity also helps students comprehend character development from the author's point of view as they work to build on a fictional character created by the author.

Grade Levels/Standards Addressed

See page 207 for the standards this strategy addresses, or refer to the Digital Resource CD (standards.pdf) to read the correlating standards in their entirety.

Stages of Writing Process

Prewrite, Draft, Revise, Edit, Publish

Activity

After reading a fictional text selection, review the importance of character development throughout the story. Make a list of characters on the board or on a sheet of chart paper, and discuss the characters' various attributes and personality traits. Display and discuss sample diary entries that showcase different writing styles and perspectives.

Make sure to highlight how the diary entries reflect the presentation of the character in the story. Ask students to choose a character from the story and write a diary entry that reflects the character's thoughts over the course of the story or a specific chapter. Instruct students to consider the following questions:

- What are the character's thoughts?

- How do the character's actions reflect his or her feelings?

- How does the character's personality and background affect the way he or she reacts to events in the story?

- How does the character react to the problem or conflict in the story?

- What are the character's feelings?

Distribute the *Character Diary* activity sheet (page 221, characterdiary.pdf) to students, and have them begin writing. Once students have written their diary entries, have them switch diary entries with partners to read other students' entries. Hold a class discussion about the various characters in the book and discuss how students were able to apply their knowledge of character development to their diary entries.

Differentiation

Provide English language learners and below-level students with sample diary entries to keep at their desks so that they can use them as models for writing their own Character Diary. These students may also benefit from the use of sentence frames to help build their entries. Above-level students should be encouraged to focus on the more complex aspects of character development. These students can use their knowledge of the character to infer the character's thoughts and feelings that are not explicitly discussed in the story and analyze the character's actions for implied motives and goals.

Character Diary

Character: _____

Date _____
_____
_____
_____
_____

Date _____
_____
_____
_____
_____

Date _____
_____
_____
_____
_____

Story Additions

Background Information

The Story Additions strategy asks students to write additional or alternative parts to an existing story. In order to do this, students must apply their knowledge of a story's characters, plot, style, and story structure in order to create a text that can be added seamlessly to the original text. This strategy can be used as a short, informal activity that can be completed during a single class period or as an extended formal writing project that lasts several days or weeks as students complete the various phases of the writing process.

Grade Levels/Standards Addressed

See page 207 for the standards this strategy addresses, or refer to the Digital Resource CD (standards.pdf) to read the correlating standards in their entirety.

Stages of Writing Process

Prewrite, Draft, Revise, Edit, Publish

Activity

Before beginning a reading selection, tell students that they will be creating additional or alternative parts (determined by the teacher prior to the activity) of the story they are about to read. Students' Story Additions can take the form of an alternative ending or beginning, an additional

chapter to add to the end of the story, or even a prequel or sequel to the text. Have students read the story independently or read it aloud to the class, and discuss the prominent literary elements that students will need to include in their story additions. Distribute the *Story Additions* activity sheet (page 223, storyadditions.pdf) to students, and ask them to fill in the information about the original text and their planned addition or alternative part. In the case of a longer writing assignment, it may also be helpful to have students use the Story Mapping strategy (see pages 199–204) before they begin writing in order to outline the relevant literary components they need to include. Once students have completed a final version of their Story Addition, provide ample opportunities for students to share their work with their peers and the school community. The Author's Chair strategy (see pages 176–179) is one effective method of sharing students' work within the classroom. To conclude the activity, ask students to reflect on the writing process and the ways in which they were able to apply their knowledge about literary concepts to their final writing product.

Differentiation

This activity demands a comprehensive understanding of the text, so it is important to choose the reading selection carefully for English language learners. It may be a good idea to use a different reading selection for English language learners and below-level students or allow these students to choose their own text on which to base their writing. Above-level students can use a more complex text.

Story Additions

Directions: Use this prewriting planner to organize your Story Addition.

Original Text

1. **Narrator:** _____

2. **Point of View:** _____

3. **Tone:** _____

4. **Setting:** _____

5. **Characters:** _____

Story Addition

Where will the text of the Story Addition occur relative to the original text (e.g., before the original text begins, in the middle, at the climax)?

_____

_____

Which characters will I include?

_____

_____

How will I make sure that the point of view and tone I use are consistent with the original text?

_____

_____

How will the events in the Story Addition connect with the plot in the original text?

_____

_____

Assessing Writing Overview

Role of Assessment of Writing in the Language Arts Classroom

The role of assessment of writing has been another reason teachers often avoid writing (Gahn 1989). However, not all writing assignments or activities in language arts need to be graded. Writing-to-learn assignments seldom need to be graded. These experiences are to provide opportunities for students to express themselves and what they are learning. The concern for how to grade more formal writing assignments can be alleviated with rubrics and checklists. These two methods can be effective and meaningful ways to assess more formal types of writing in the classroom. Writing assessments will be described and discussed in detail in the last section of this book.

Authentic Assessment of Writing

Views of teaching and learning have changed to include the concept of *constructivism*—the belief that learners actively and dynamically construct the information they are learning about the world. The learner is not an "empty cup" to be filled with knowledge and information. Constructivism holds a view that learning includes and incorporates a dynamic and active mental process (e.g., Jones et al. 1987; Marzano, Pickering, and McTighe 1993; Resnick and Klopfer 1989). Students learn through interactive and integrative experiences in the classroom; the more a student actively listens, speaks, reads, writes, and thinks, the easier the learning and retention of knowledge will be.

There is a variety of ways to construct knowledge and learn (Pressley 1990; Weinstein and Mayer 1986), but one of the key ways to help learning occur is to have students write.

Although many teachers agree with the notion of interactive learning, they feel inadequate when grading or assessing this type of learning. For example, how does a teacher assign a grade to something that is not formal writing? How does the teacher assess the learning of literary skills and concepts through writing? These concerns are valid. Assessment of this type of writing must validate learning, and it must acknowledge the language arts standards and objectives as well. Authentic assessment reflects back on the meaningful instruction and learning process. There are many different types of authentic assessment of writing done in the classroom (Feuer and Fulton 1993).

Incorporating authentic assessment in the classroom requires little time, effort, or experience. It is not uncommon for a teacher to feel uncomfortable grading students' informal writing, but they may realize that they are already using some types of authentic assessment in their classroom. The types of authentic assessments that lend themselves to writing in the language arts classroom include holistic assessment, primary trait assessment, and analytic scoring (Cohen 1994; Herman, Aschbacher, and Winters 1992).

Self-assessment and peer assessments provide opportunities for students to reflect on their own writing abilities as well as their understanding of literary concepts. Peer assessment also provides other examples of writing for students to read and compare and contrast with their own writing and understanding. The portfolio assessment strategy also represents a unique evaluative technique that allows the teacher to gauge the progress and improvement of a student's writing skills over a designated time period.

Assessing Writing Overview *(cont.)*

Standards Addressed

The following chart shows the correlating standards for each strategy in this section. Refer to the Digital Resource CD (standards.pdf) to read the correlating standards in their entirety.

Strategy	McREL Standards	Common Core State Standards
Holistic Assessment	Grades 1–2 (1.4) Grades 3–5 (1.4) Grades 6–8 (1.4) Grades 9–12 (1.4)	Grade 1 (W.1.5) Grade 2 (W.2.5) Grade 3 (W.3.5) Grade 4 (W.4.5) Grade 5 (W.5.5) Grade 6 (W.6.5) Grade 7 (W.7.5) Grade 8 (W.8.5) Grades 9–10 (W.9–10.5) Grades 11–12 (W.11–12.5)
Analytic Assessment	Grades 1–2 (1.4) Grades 3–5 (1.4) Grades 6–8 (1.4) Grades 9–12 (1.4)	Grade 1 (W.1.5) Grade 2 (W.2.5) Grade 3 (W.3.5) Grade 4 (W.4.5) Grade 5 (W.5.5) Grade 6 (W.6.5) Grade 7 (W.7.5) Grade 8 (W.8.5) Grades 9–10 (W.9–10.5) Grades 11–12 (W.11–12.5)
Primary Trait Assessment	Grades 1–2 (1.4) Grades 3–5 (1.4) Grades 6–8 (1.4) Grades 9–12 (1.4)	Grade 1 (W.1.5) Grade 2 (W.2.5) Grade 3 (W.3.5) Grade 4 (W.4.5) Grade 5 (W.5.5) Grade 6 (W.6.5) Grade 7 (W.7.5) Grade 8 (W.8.5) Grades 9–10 (W.9–10.5) Grades 11–12 (W.11–12.5)

Assessing Writing Overview (cont.)

Strategy	McREL Standards	Common Core State Standards
Self-Assessment	Grades 1–2 (1.4) Grades 3–5 (1.4) Grades 6–8 (1.4) Grades 9–12 (1.4)	Grade 1 (W.1.5) Grade 2 (W.2.5) Grade 3 (W.3.5) Grade 4 (W.4.5) Grade 5 (W.5.5) Grade 6 (W.6.5) Grade 7 (W.7.5) Grade 8 (W.8.5) Grades 9–10 (W.9–10.5) Grades 11–12 (W.11–12.5)
Peer Assessment	Grades 1–2 (1.4) Grades 3–5 (1.4) Grades 6–8 (1.4) Grades 9–12 (1.4)	Grade 1 (W.1.5) Grade 2 (W.2.5) Grade 3 (W.3.5) Grade 4 (W.4.5) Grade 5 (W.5.5) Grade 6 (W.6.5) Grade 7 (W.7.5) Grade 8 (W.8.5) Grades 9–10 (W.9–10.5) Grades 11–12 (W.11–12.5)
Teacher Conference	Grades 1–2 (1.4) Grades 3–5 (1.4) Grades 6–8 (1.4) Grades 9–12 (1.4)	Grade 1 (W.1.5) Grade 2 (W.2.5) Grade 3 (W.3.5) Grade 4 (W.4.5) Grade 5 (W.5.5) Grade 6 (W.6.5) Grade 7 (W.7.5) Grade 8 (W.8.5) Grades 9–10 (W.9–10.5) Grades 11–12 (W.11–12.5)
Portfolio Assessment	Grades 1–2 (1.4) Grades 3–5 (1.4) Grades 6–8 (1.4) Grades 9–12 (1.4)	Grade 1 (W.1.5) Grade 2 (W.2.5) Grade 3 (W.3.5) Grade 4 (W.4.5) Grade 5 (W.5.5) Grade 6 (W.6.5) Grade 7 (W.7.5) Grade 8 (W.8.5) Grades 9–10 (W.9–10.5) Grades 11–12 (W.11–12.5)

Holistic Assessment

Background Information

Holistic Assessment evaluates the overall picture of the writing as opposed to the individual writing components. This assessment uses a list of criteria that are analyzed to produce one score on a scale of 1–6. The criteria, which address both language arts objectives and writing skills, are determined prior to the assignment, and the student is informed of the criteria before writing takes place. The criteria can be adapted to meet students' needs and the objectives of the assignment. The four main criteria are as follows:

- Idea Development/Organization—Does the student communicate a central idea or purpose? Has this idea been supported throughout the piece, and is there a conclusion?

- Fluency/Structure—Does the student use correct grammar (verb endings, verb tenses, pronouns, etc.) and syntax in the writing?

- Word Choice—Does the student incorporate a variety of words and content-specific terms?

- Mechanics—Does the student use correct spelling, capitalization, and punctuation?

The objective of this assessment is for students to develop and strengthen their writing by planning, revising, and editing. By implementing this strategy prior to assigning a writing assignment, students can plan and revise their work based on clear expectations and guidelines.

Grade Levels/Standards Addressed

See page 225 for the standards this strategy addresses, or refer to the Digital Resource CD (standards.pdf) to read the correlating standards in their entirety.

Stage of Writing Process

Reflection

Activity

Prior to beginning a writing assignment, distribute the *Holistic Assessment* activity sheet (page 228, holistic.pdf) to students, and review and discuss it. Please note that this rubric can be altered to fit the needs of the writing assignment and the age of students. Be sure that they are clear on the expectations of the writing assignment and on how they will be assessed prior to beginning the writing. You may also choose to include students in creating the criteria. After students complete the writing, pair each student with a partner to exchange the writing, and provide suggestions, comments, and feedback. Then, collect students' writing and use the rubric to rate each piece with a score from 1–6.

Differentiation

Adapt the rubric to meet the needs of English language learners and their abilities. They may not be expected to meet the grade-level expectations in grammar and mechanics, for example. Challenge above-level students to create their own criteria and rubric. Help below-level students use the rubric throughout the writing process to meet the expectations.

Name: _____ **Date:** _____

Holistic Assessment

Title: _____

Topic: _____

Level 6—Writing conveys clear meaning and ideas.
• organizes the piece with several paragraphs, and develops ideas and a conclusion • incorporates smooth transitions • incorporates necessary language arts concepts and ideas • uses a variety of vocabulary words, including literary vocabulary and terms • writing has few or no grammatical or mechanical errors
Level 5—Writing conveys meaning and ideas.
• organizes the piece with several paragraphs, though some portions may not be fully developed • incorporates some smooth transitions • incorporates some language arts concepts and ideas • uses some literary vocabulary and terms • writing has some grammatical or mechanical errors
Level 4—Writing expresses an idea most of the time.
• develops a cohesive paragraph • uses a variety of sentence structures with few transitions • selects some language arts vocabulary and terms • writing has some grammatical or mechanical errors
Level 3—Begins to write about an idea but fails to support it.
• sometimes develops a cohesive paragraph • uses complete sentences • incorporates few language arts vocabulary and terms • writing has many grammatical or mechanical errors
Level 2—Attempts to write about an idea.
• there are no cohesive paragraphs • uses complete sentences sometimes • lack of language arts vocabulary and terms incorporated in writing • writing has multiple grammatical or mechanical errors
Level 1—There is no common theme or idea.
• sentences are written but are incomplete • uses sentences with few transitions • language arts vocabulary and terms are not used • writing has too many grammatical or mechanical errors

Analytic Assessment

Background Information

With Analytic Assessment, each component of the writing is analyzed independently of the others and given its own score. The writing assignment is given several scores, each representing the different components. The teacher may also choose to weigh one component more heavily than another to add emphasis. Analytic assessment not only allows the teacher to provide specific feedback to students but it also helps the teacher target certain areas in planning, instruction, and assessment (Perkins 1983).

The objective of this assessment is for students to develop and strengthen their writing by planning, revising, and editing. By implementing this strategy prior to assigning a writing assignment, students can plan and revise their work based on clear expectations and guidelines.

Grade Levels/Standards Addressed

See page 225 for the standards this strategy addresses, or refer to the Digital Resource CD (standards.pdf) to read the correlating standards in their entirety.

Stage of Writing Process

Reflection

Activity

Working together with students, create a rubric that scores each component of the writing assignment. The writing components may include composition, mechanics, sentence formation, language arts content, and usage. Determine if one component of the rubric should receive more emphasis than another. Determine the number of points scored for each component. Review the *Analytic Assessment* activity sheet (page 230, analytic.pdf) with students prior to giving instructions on the writing assignment. Be sure students understand how they will be graded. Show models of writing samples. Allow time for students to complete the writing assignment, and then compare it to the designated rubric. Students can then edit and make changes as they deem necessary. Use the *Analytic Assessment* activity sheet to score students' writing assignments.

Differentiation

Work independently with English language learners to create a rubric that meets their specific needs to ensure a greater chance of success. If desired, include a component of writing in English as part of the rubric. Encourage above-level students to create their own rubrics, score their writing assignments, and compare them with the scores you determined for the writing. You may also weigh certain components more heavily to challenge above-level students. If appropriate, adapt rubrics for below-level students to address their individual needs.

Name: _____ **Date:** _____

Analytic Assessment

Title: _____

Topic: _____

Skill	Excellent (3 points)	Satisfactory (2 points)	Needs Improvement (1 point)
Stays on topic			
Shows a clear purpose (topic sentence)			
Includes supporting details with specific examples			
Has sequential and/or logical development			
Includes a main idea paragraph			
Clearly presents concepts			
Expresses ideas clearly			
Uses complete sentences			
Uses varied sentence types and structures			
Uses vocabulary words correctly			
Uses correct spelling			

Comments: _____

_____

_____

_____

#51006—*Writing Strategies for Fiction*

Primary Trait Assessment

Background Information

Primary Trait Assessment is a way for the teacher to focus on one specific skill or trait. The teacher determines the skill, trait, or feature that will be analyzed and assessed in a piece of writing. The trait can be writing–based or content–based, depending on the intent of the lesson. In primary trait writing, only the primary trait is scored. The other traits and elements are ignored.

A benefit of using the Primary Trait Assessment is that students may feel more at ease with the primary trait focus because they can focus on one area. Teachers, too, can focus on specific areas of concern. The Primary Trait Assessment also allows the teacher to focus specifically on the language arts skill or concept (e.g., theme, symbolism, etc.) while ignoring the mechanics and other areas of writing. With any rubric, clearly communicate the goals and expectations prior to assigning a writing task.

The objective of this assessment is for students to develop and strengthen their writing by planning, revising, and editing. By implementing this strategy prior to assigning a writing assignment, students can plan and revise their work based on clear expectations and guidelines.

Grade Levels/Standards Addressed

See page 225 for the standards this strategy addresses, or refer to the Digital Resource CD (standards.pdf) to read the correlating standards in their entirety.

Stage of Writing Process

Reflection

Activity

Determine the writing assignment to be used for the Primary Trait Assessment rubric for scoring. Select the specific trait or skill that you would like students to focus on during the writing assignment. Display the *Primary Trait Assessment* activity sheet (page 232, primarytrait.pdf) for students to see before they begin writing. Tell students the primary trait that is the focus for this writing assignment. Explain that the other areas of writing will be ignored for assessment purposes. Allow time for students to draft and edit their writing before submitting it for assessment. If desired, pair students with partners to edit one another's writing. When using the *Primary Trait Assessment* activity sheet, be sure to give specific feedback on how students can improve in this primary trait. Use this rubric the next time students write so that you can look for progress on the primary trait.

Differentiation

Select a primary trait for English language learners to fit their specific language needs. Challenge above-level students by selecting a primary trait that is not a clear strength, and have them decide how to improve their area of focus. Give specific feedback to below-level students on what they need to improve, and encourage them to revise and edit their work. Design a specific primary trait focus that will meet their individual needs.

Name: _____ **Date:** _____

Primary Trait Assessment

Title: _____

Topic: _____

Select the primary trait for focus and use the following rubric (with adjustments, if needed) to assess students' writing. Leave specific feedback.

5 The student demonstrates desired skills throughout the text.

4 Most of the time, the student demonstrates desired skills in the text.

3 Occasionally, the student demonstrates desired skills in the text.

2 Seldom does the student demonstrate desired skills in the text.

1 The student is not using desired skills in the text.

_____ **Content:**
The writer presents a main point and uses a clear organizational structure. The writer presents information logically. The writer anticipates and addresses the concerns and questions of the reader. The writer cites sources of information whenever necessary. The writer uses books and other resources to gather information. The writer conveys an intended purpose in writing. The writer understands and portrays the language arts concepts in a meaningful way.
Comments: _____

_____ **Writing Conventions:**
The writer has taken time and effort to ensure the writing does not have spelling errors. Each sentence begins with a capital and ends with the correct punctuation. The writing contains clear transitions to convey ideas. Each paragraph of the writing is dedicated to only one idea. The report contains no mechanical errors. The writing is ready to publish.
Comments: _____

_____ **Use of Language:**
The writer creates a structure appropriate to the needs of a specific audience. The writer uses descriptive language that clarifies and enhances ideas. The writer engages the reader. The writer expresses an individual, consistent voice. The writer uses an interesting lead.
Comments: _____

_____ **Organization/Structure:**
The writing is organized and follows the recommended structure for a report. The parts of a report (title, main idea, examples to support the main idea, and summary or conclusion) are present. The report is at least five paragraphs in length.
Comments: _____

Self-Assessment

Background Information

Self-Assessment is a way for students to assess their own work. Students learn to look critically at their own work and analyze it for strengths and weaknesses. A benefit of using Self-Assessment is that students take ownership of the assessment process, which personalizes the learning for them. Some students who are extremely sensitive about receiving feedback may appreciate this method of assessment. Also, teachers can use student reflections as a springboard into developing personal goals for students. Having a personal goal to strive toward will make future writing assignments more meaningful.

The objective of this assessment is for students to develop and strengthen their writing by planning, revising, and editing. By implementing this strategy prior to assigning a writing assignment, students can plan and revise their work based on clear expectations and guidelines.

Grade Levels/Standards Addressed

See page 226 for the standards this strategy addresses, or refer to the Digital Resource CD (standards.pdf) to read the correlating standards in their entirety.

Stage of Writing Process

Reflection

Activity

Determine the writing assignment to be used for Self-Assessment. Display the *Self-Assessment* activity sheets (pages 234–235, selfassessment.pdf) for students to see before they begin writing. Tell students that they will be responsible for evaluating their own writing when they have completed the writing assignment. Encourage students to refer to the checklist and survey throughout the writing process so that they keep the goals in mind as they work. For students who may be unaccustomed to using Self-Assessment, consider allowing them to work in pairs to "practice" completing the checklist and survey before they have officially published their work. This may help them look more critically at their own work before the final evaluation. After students have completed their Self-Assessment checklist and survey, take time to conference individually to provide constructive feedback and set goals for the next writing piece. When work begins on the following assignment, ask students to identify one or two elements on the checklist where they would like to improve.

Differentiation

Consider limiting the elements on the checklist for English language learners and below-level students while still maintaining a focus on using and applying the grade-appropriate language arts content. English language learners will need the checklist adapted to meet their specific needs so the expectations are appropriate for their current level of language development. Below-level students may focus on one or two elements in each category so that they are not overwhelmed. Challenge above-level students to apply higher-level writing strategies, use more advanced vocabulary, and incorporate more complex sentence structures. Replace simplistic items on their checklists with more complex items in areas where they can work on developing their skills to ensure they are appropriately challenged.

Name: _____ Date: _____

Self-Assessment

Title: _____

Topic: _____

Directions: Answer the questions below to self-assess your writing.

1. **Capitalization**

   _____ Did I capitalize the first word of each sentence?

   _____ Did I capitalize proper nouns such as names and places?

2. **Punctuation**

   _____ Did I put a ., !, or a ? at the end of each sentence?

   _____ Did I use commas in a series?

   _____ Did I use commas in dates?

   _____ Have I been careful not to use the exclamation point too much?

   _____ Have I used quotation marks when I needed them?

3. **Handwriting**

   _____ Did I write neatly?

   _____ Are there missing words that need to be added?

   _____ Are there extra words that need to be deleted?

4. **Spelling**

   _____ Did I check my spelling?

5. **Overall Content**

   _____ Have I been clear about the topic of my writing?

   _____ Is it easy to tell what the main idea is?

   _____ Have I used any special words or phrases that add to my writing?

   _____ Are there any words or phrases that are confusing?

   _____ Have I used an interesting lead?

   _____ Have I considered what would make my writing better?

6. **Language Arts Content**

   _____ Did I use the correct literary terms?

   _____ Did I write about the language arts topic accurately?

   _____ Did I do adequate research on the language arts topic?

   _____ Did I use my own words?

   _____ Do I clearly understand the language arts topic I am writing about?

Self-Assessment *(cont.)*

I think this writing piece shows that I can…

_____

_____

_____

One thing I learned from writing this is…

_____

_____

_____

I have improved my writing in these areas…

_____

_____

_____

The next time I write, I will…

_____

_____

_____

Did I give my best to this writing assignment? Why or why not?

_____

_____

_____

Peer Assessment

Background Information

Peer Assessment is a way for students to practice analyzing the work of others. Students learn to look critically at others' work and analyze it for strengths and weaknesses. This strategy also enables students to deepen their understanding of the expectations of each particular writing genre. In order to assess their peers' work, students must have a comprehensive understanding of the topic themselves. As with Self-Assessment, students take ownership of the assessment process with Peer Assessment—even though they are not assessing their own work—which personalizes the learning for them. This assessment tool can be used in conjunction with another, such as Teacher Conference, or a traditional rubric. Teachers can also ask students to reflect on what they saw in their partners' work and choose an aspect that they might want to include in their own writing in the future.

The objective of this assessment is for students to develop and strengthen their writing by planning, revising, and editing. By implementing this strategy prior to assigning a writing assignment, students can plan and revise their work based on clear expectations and guidelines.

Grade Levels/Standards Addressed

See page 226 for the standards this strategy addresses, or refer to the Digital Resource CD (standards.pdf) to read the correlating standards in their entirety.

Stage of Writing Process

Reflection

Activity

Determine the writing assignment to be used for Peer Assessment. Display the *Peer Assessment* activity sheet (page 237, peerassessment.pdf) before students begin writing, and model how to complete it with a sample piece of writing. In order to make this a positive process, provide explicit examples of feedback and constructive criticism so that students are clear on how they are to evaluate a classmates' work. Tell students that they will be responsible for evaluating their peers' writing when they have completed the writing assignment. Encourage students to keep their audience in mind as they work. After all students have completed their writing, distribute the activity sheet and assign partners. Have students read their partners' work and add their comments to the assessment. You may wish to collect the Peer Assessment sheets to screen the partners' comments or add your own comments before returning them to students with their written work.

Differentiation

Preteach English language learners how to use the activity sheet as well as the language they will need to respond. Also, consider how to instruct these students' partners about responding to the writing of English language learners so that their comments are directed toward the expectations of their individual language levels. Adjust their response prompts, if needed. Below-level students may not need differentiation to complete the activity, but their partners may need some guidance on how to respond. Consider altering the checklists for these students' writing to address their levels of proficiency. Have above-level students work in small groups to evaluate their writing based on higher-level prompts, and ask them to provide examples to support their feedback and suggestions.

Name: _____ **Date:** _____

Peer Assessment

Author's Name: _____

Title: _____ **Topic:** _____

Mark an *X* in the appropriate column:	Very Much	Somewhat
1. I enjoyed reading this piece of writing.	_____	_____
2. I think this writing is easy to read.	_____	_____
3. The writing is creative.	_____	_____
4. The writing made sense to me.	_____	_____

Finish the following statements as best you can. Remember, your job is to help the writer.

1. One thing I really like about this writing is…

_____

2. One thing I think the author can improve upon is…

_____

3. Something I would like to tell the author is…

_____

4. I think other people who will read this piece will think…

_____

5. One thing that I can learn from the author and this writing is…

_____

Teacher Conference

Background Information

Teachers are often frustrated and disappointed when students' writing assignments are turned in off topic, disorganized, or lacking the proper amount of information. Teacher Conferences allow teachers to maintain consistent communication with their students throughout the writing process. These opportunities, although brief, can keep students on track and give them the scaffolds and suggestions they need to create better pieces of writing. It is important for teachers to also take the time in these conferences to ask questions of students and listen to what challenges they might be facing so students feel that the conferences are less evaluative and more cooperative.

Grade Levels/Standards Addressed

See page 226 for the standards this strategy addresses, or refer to the Digital Resource CD (standards.pdf) to read the correlating standards in their entirety.

Stage of Writing Process

Reflection

Activity

Determine the writing assignment to be used for Teacher Conferences. Display the *Teacher Conference* activity sheet (page 239, teacherconference.pdf) for students to see before they begin writing. Tell students that they will be meeting with you at each phase of the writing process to discuss their writing, share concerns, ask for suggestions, and receive feedback. Students should keep their copy of the activity sheet with them as they write. Encourage them to refer to the form throughout the writing process so that they keep the goals of each phase in mind as they work. As you guide students through each phase of the writing process, take time to conference individually to provide constructive feedback and set goals for the next phase. When their writing assignment is complete, be sure to add clear, explicit feedback so that students have a clear understanding of the strengths and weaknesses of their work. When students begin the next assignment, ask them to identify one or two elements on the checklist where they would like to improve.

Differentiation

Consider limiting the elements on the checklist for English language learners and below-level students while still maintaining a focus of using and applying the grade-appropriate language arts content. English language learners will need the checklist adapted to develop expectations that are appropriate for their current level of language development. Below-level students may focus on one or two elements in each category so that they do not get overwhelmed. Above-level students should be challenged to apply higher-level writing strategies, use more advanced vocabulary, and incorporate more complex sentence structures. Their checklists can also be revised to include areas where they are still developing their skills to ensure that they are appropriately challenged.

Name: _____ **Date:** _____

Teacher Conference

Title: _____

Topic: _____

	Needs Work	Good	Excellent
Brainstorming			
The writing is well thought out.	_____	_____	_____
The writing is easy to follow.	_____	_____	_____
The writing is creative and interesting.	_____	_____	_____
Drafting			
The writing is organized.	_____	_____	_____
The writing uses the correct format.	_____	_____	_____
The writing is complete.	_____	_____	_____
Editing and Revising			
The writing has complete sentences.	_____	_____	_____
The writing uses correct punctuation.	_____	_____	_____
The writing uses capitalization correctly.	_____	_____	_____
The writing uses correct spelling.	_____	_____	_____
The writing uses transition words.	_____	_____	_____
Publishing			
The writing is written or typed neatly.	_____	_____	_____
The writing has a capitalized title.	_____	_____	_____
The writing has been illustrated, if needed.	_____	_____	_____

Teacher Comments

Your writing is very good in these ways: _____

_____

_____

Your writing could be made better by doing these things: _____

_____

_____

Portfolio Assessment

Background Information

The Portfolio Assessment strategy is a longitudinal tool used to assess the development of students' writing skills over a period of time. When using this assessment strategy, students compile a collection of personal writing samples from a specific period of learning (e.g., grading period, literature unit) and then choose the pieces that they want to include in their portfolio. Students complete written reflections for each piece, outlining the purpose the piece plays in the portfolio, and then the teacher assesses the portfolio using students' writing samples and reflections. This assessment technique gives students the decision-making power to choose which pieces will be included in the portfolio, thereby fostering student ownership over their writing (Genesee and Upshur 1996). Furthermore, the longitudinal nature of this assessment strategy allows students to demonstrate how their writing skills have grown over time and understand that they are assessed on their progress rather than the final writing product.

Grade Levels/Standards Addressed

See page 226 for the standards this strategy addresses, or refer to the Digital Resource CD (standards.pdf) to read the correlating standards in their entirety.

Stage of Writing Process

Reflection

Activity

In order to use the Portfolio Assessment strategy, students must first compile a collection of writing samples over the course of a designated time period. For younger students, it may be easier for the teacher to keep these collections in student folders in the classroom while older students compile their own collections. Once students have collected a series of writing samples, explain that they need to choose a set number of pieces (e.g., five) upon which they will be assessed. Encourage students to choose the pieces that they feel showcase their best writing samples. If students have samples that include multiple drafts, ask them to include all of the drafts as evidence of their writing improvement and progress. The teacher may also choose to add other guidelines for selecting writing samples (e.g., students must choose one piece of writing from each genre). Once students have chosen the pieces to include, they complete the *Student Writing Sample Reflection* activity sheet (page 241, writingreflection.pdf) for each piece, explaining their reasoning behind choosing this particular piece. The portfolio is then assessed by the teacher using the *Portfolio Assessment* activity sheet (page 242, portfolioassessment.pdf). If possible, provide students with the opportunity to share their portfolios with their peers, teachers, and parents through student-led conferences.

Differentiation

Make sure that English language learners understand the guidelines for choosing portfolio writing samples, and provide them with samples of the type of work that they should include. It may also be helpful for these students to work with a partner to choose the pieces for their portfolio so they can practice discussing their reasoning before they complete the reflections. Above-level students should be challenged to critically evaluate their own work and to provide evidence of learning and improvement through their portfolio. Below-level students may need assistance in choosing pieces for their portfolio and completing the written reflections. Individual or small-group conferences with the teacher will help guide these students through the process.

Student Writing Sample Reflection

Author's Name: _____

Writing Assignment: _____

1. I chose this writing assignment because...

_____

_____

_____

2. Two things I want others to notice about my writing include...

_____

_____

_____

3. This piece of writing shows improvement or progress because...

_____

_____

_____

4. I have/have not chosen to revise this piece because...

_____

_____

_____

5. The next time I complete a similar writing assignment, my goal will be to...

_____

_____

_____

Name: _____ **Date:** _____

Portfolio Assessment

Student Name: _____ **Date:** _____

Teacher Name: _____

Criteria	Improvement Needed	Somewhat Disagree	Somewhat Agree	Excellent
1. The portfolio includes the correct number and type of writing samples.				
2. The portfolio includes a reflection for each writing sample.				
3. The portfolio is well organized/well presented.				
4. The student consistently strives to improve writing.				
5. The portfolio reveals student improvement and progress in writing.				
6. The portfolio shows evidence of personal reflection.				
7. The student demonstrates awareness of personal strengths and weaknesses.				

Teacher Comments:

_____

_____

_____

_____

_____

_____

_____

References Cited

Adams, Marilyn Jager. 1990. *Beginning to Read: Thinking and Learning about Print.* Cambridge, MA: Massachusetts Institute of Technology.

Allyn, Pam. 2013. *Be Core Ready: Powerful, Effective Steps to Implementing and Achieving the Common Core State Standards.* Upper Saddle River, NJ: Pearson Education.

Anderson, Richard C., and Peter Freebody. 1985. "Vocabulary Knowledge." In *Theoretical Models and Processes of Reading.* 3rd edition. Edited by Harry Singer and Robert B. Ruddell. Newark, DE: International Reading Association, 343–371.

Angelo, Thomas A., and K. Patricia Cross. 1993. *Classroom Assessment Techniques: A Handbook for College Teachers.* 2nd edition. San Francisco, CA: Jossey-Bass.

Atwell, Nancie. 1984. "Writing and Reading Literature from the Inside Out." *Language Arts* 61 (3): 240–252.

Barr, Mary A., and Mary K. Healy. 1988. "School and University Articulation: Different Contexts for Writing Across the Curriculum." *New Directions for Teaching and Learning* 36 (Winter): 43–53.

Bean, John C. 1996. "Helping Students Read Difficult Texts." In *Engaging Ideas: The Professor's Guide to Integrating Writing, Critical Thinking, and Active Learning in the Classroom.* San Francisco, CA: Jossey-Bass, 133–147.

Becker, Wesley C. 1977. "Teaching Reading and Language to the Disadvantaged—What We Have Learned from Field Research." *Harvard Educational Review* 47 (4): 518–543.

Bintz, William P. 2011. "Teaching Vocabulary Across the Curriculum." *Middle School Journal* 42 (4): 44–53.

Boutwell, Marilyn A. 1983. "Reading and Writing: A Reciprocal Agreement." *Language Arts* 60 (6): 723–730.

Bringle, Robert G., and Julie A. Hatcher. 1996. "Reflection Activities for the College Classroom." Paper presented at the National Gathering on June 21.

Britton, James, Tony Burgess, Nancy Martin, Alex McLeod, and Harold Rosen. 1975. *The Development of Writing Abilities,* 11–18. New York: Macmillan Education.

Brozo, William G., and Michele L. Simpson. 2003. *Readers, Teachers, Learners: Expanding Literacy Across the Content Areas.* 4th edition. Upper Saddle River, NJ: Merrill.

Buehl, Doug. 2008. *Classroom Strategies for Interactive Learning.* 3rd edition. Newark, DE: International Reading Association.

References Cited (cont.)

Calkins, Lucy McCormick. 1983. *Lessons from a Child: On the Teaching and Learning of Writing.* Portsmouth, NH: Heinemann.

Calkins, Lucy, Amanda Hartman, and Zoë White. 2005. *One to One: The Art of Conferring with Young Writers.* Portsmouth, NH: Heinemann.

Calkins, Lucy, Mary Ehrenworth, and Christopher Lehman. 2012. *Pathways to the Common Core: Accelerating Acheivement.* Portsmouth, NH: Heinemann.

Carey-Webb, Allen. 2001. *Literature and Lives: A Response-Based, Cultural Studies Approach to Teaching English.* Urbana, IL: National Council of Teachers of English.

Chamot, Anna Uhl, and J. Michael O'Malley. 1994. *The CALLA Handbook.* Reading, MA: Addison-Wesley.

Christen, William L., and Thomas J. Murphy. 1991. "Increasing Comprehension by Activating Prior Knowledge." ERIC Digest. Bloomington, IN: ERIC Clearinghouse on Reading, English, and Communication. ERIC Identifier: ED328885.

Cohen, Andrew D. 1994. *Assessing Language Ability in the Classroom.* 2nd edition. Boston, MA: Heinle and Heinle.

Combs, Warren E. 2012. *Writer's Workshop for the Common Core: A Step-by-Step Guide.* Larchmont, NY: Eye on Education.

Corona, Cathy, Sandra Spangenberger, and Iris Venet. 1998. "Improving Student Writing through a Language Rich Environment." M.A. Action Research Project, St. Xavier University and IRI/Skylight, 61 pages.

Dechant, Emerald. 1991. *Understanding and Teaching Reading: An Interactive Model.* Hillsdale, NJ: Lawrence Erlbaum.

Dingli, Alexiei. 2011. *Knowledge Annotation: Making Implicit Knowledge Explicit.* Berlin: Springer-Verlag.

Duke, Nell K., and P. David Pearson. 2001. "Developing Comprehension in the Primary Grades." A Presentation to the International Reading Association. http://www.ciera.org/library/presos/2001/2001IRA/ira01ddp.pdf.

Dunlap, Carmen Zuñiga, and Evelyn Marino Weisman. 2006. *Helping English Language Learners Succeed.* Huntington Beach, CA: Shell Education.

Eanet, Marilyn G., and Anthony V. Manzo. 1976. "REAP—A Strategy for Improving Reading/Writing/Study Skills." *Journal of Reading* 19 (8): 647–652.

References Cited (cont.)

Elbow, Peter. 1973. *Writing Without Teachers*. New York: Oxford University Press.

Emig, Janet. 1977. "Writing as a Mode of Learning." *College Composition and Communication* 28 (2): 122–128.

Feuer, Michael J., and Kathleen Fulton. 1993. "The Many Faces of Performance Assessment." *Phi Delta Kappan* 74 (6): 478.

Fink, Rosalie. 2006. *Why Jane and John Couldn't Read—And How They Learned*. Newark, DE: International Reading Association.

Fisher, Douglas, and Gay Ivey. 2005. "Literacy and Language as Learning in Content Area Classes: A Departure from 'Every Teacher a Teacher of Reading.'" *Action in Teacher Education* 27 (2): 3–11.

Fisher, Douglas, and Nancy Frey. 2004. *Improving Adolescent Literacy: Content Area Strategies at Work*. Upper Saddle River, NJ: Pearson Education.

Frayer, Dorothy A., Wayne C. Fredrick, and Herbert J. Klausmeier. 1969. "A Schema for Testing the Level of Concept Mastery. Working Paper No. 16." Madison, WI: Wisconsin Research and Development Center for Cognitive Learning.

Fulwiler, Toby. 1980. "Journals across the Disciplines." *English Journal* 69 (12): 14–19.

Gahn, Shelley Mattson. 1989. "A practical guide for teaching and writing in the content areas." *Journal of Reading* 32 (6): 525–531.

Genesee, Fred, and John A. Upshur. 1996. *Classroom-Based Evaluation in Second Language Education*. New York: Cambridge University Press.

Gentry, J. Richard. 2006. *Breaking the Code: The New Science of Beginning Reading and Writing*. Portsmouth, NH: Heinemann.

Goldman, Susan R., Jason L. G. Braasch, Jennifer Wiley, Arthur C. Graesser, and Kamila Brodowinska. 2012. "Comprehending and Learning From Internet Sources: Processing Patterns of Better and Poorer Learners." *Reading Research Quarterly* 47 (4): 356–381.

Graves, Donald H. 1983. *Writing: Teachers & Children at Work*. Portsmouth, NH: Heinemann.

Graves, Donald H., and Jane Hansen. 1983. "The Author's Chair." *Language Arts* 60 (2): 176–83.

Greenberg, Joel, and Christine Rath. 1985. "Empowering Students through Writing." *Educational Leadership* 42 (5): 10–13.

References Cited (cont.)

Haggard, Martha Rapp. 1982. "The Vocabulary Self-Collection Strategy: An Active Approach to Word Learning." *Journal of Reading* 26 (3): 203–207.

Haggard, Martha Rapp. 1986. "The Vocabulary Self-Collection Strategy: Using Student Interest and World Knowledge to Enhance Vocabulary Growth." *Journal of Reading* 29 (7): 634–642.

Hamilton-Wieler, Sharon. 1988. "Writing as a Thought Process: Site of a Struggle." *Journal of Teaching Writing* 7 (2): 167–180.

Hamilton-Wieler, Sharon. 1989. "Awkward Compromises and Eloquent Achievements." *English Education* 21 (3): 152–169.

Hamp-Lyons, Elizabeth. 1983. "Developing a Course to Teach Extensive Reading Skills to University-Bound ESL Learners." *System 11* (3): 303–312.

Harste, Jerome C., Kathy G. Short, and Carolyn Burke. 1988. *Creating Classrooms for Authors: The Reading-Writing Connection*. Portsmouth, NH: Heinemann.

Harvey, Stephanie. 1998. *Nonfiction Matters: Reading, Writing, and Research in Grades 3–8*. Portland, ME: Stenhouse Publishers.

Hefflin, Bena R., and Douglas K. Hartman. 2002. "Using Writing to Improve Comprehension: A Review of the Writing-to-Reading Research." In *Improving Comprehension Instruction: Rethinking Research, Theory, and Classroom Practice*, edited by Cathy Collins Block, Linda B. Gambrell, and Michael Pressley. San Francisco, CA: Jossey-Bass, 199–228.

Herman, Joan L., Pamela R. Aschbacher, and Lynn Winters. 1992. *A Practical Guide to Alternative Assessment*. Alexandria, VA: Association for Supervision and Curriculum Development.

Hightshue, Deborah, Dott Ryan, Sally McKenna, Joe Tower, and Brenda Brumley. 1988. "Writing in Junior and Senior High Schools." *Phi Delta Kappan* 69 (10): 725–728.

Hoyt, Jeff E. 1999. "Remedial Education and Student Attrition." *Community College Review* 27 (2): 51–73.

Huba, Mary E., and Jann E. Freed. 2000. "Using Rubrics to Provide Feedback to Students." In *Learner-Centered Assessment on College Campuses: Shifting the Focus from Teaching to Learning*. Needham Heights, MA: Allyn & Bacon, 151–200.

Johns, Jerry L., and Roberta L. Berglund. 2010. *Strategies for Content Area Learning*. Dubuque, IA: Kendall Hunt Publishing.

References Cited (cont.)

Jones, Beau Fly, Annemarie Sullivan Palincsar, Donna Sederburg Ogle, and Eileen Glynn Carr, eds. 1987. *Strategic Teaching and Learning: Cognitive Instruction in the Content Areas.* Alexandria, VA: Association of Supervision and Curriculum Development.

Karelitz, Ellen Blackburn. 1982. "The Rhythm of Writing Development." In *Understanding Writing: Ways of Observing, Learning, and Teaching.* Edited by Nancie Atwell and Thomas Newkirk. Chelmsford, MA: Northeast Regional Exchange.

Laflamme, John G. 1997. "The Effect of Multiple Exposure Vocabulary Method and the Target Reading/ Writing Strategy on Test Scores." *Journal of Adolescent & Adult Literacy* 40 (5): 372–384.

Lenski, Susan Davis, Mary Ann Wham, and Jerry L. Johns. 1999. *Reading & Learning Strategies for Middle & High School Students.* Dubuque, IA: Kendall/Hunt.

Maria, Katherine. 1990. *Reading Comprehension Instruction: Issues & Strategies.* Parkton, MD: York Press.

Marzano, Robert J., Debra J. Pickering, and Jay McTighe. 1993. *Assessing Student Outcomes: Performance Assessment Using the Dimensions of Learning Model.* Alexandria, VA: Association for Supervision and Curriculum Development.

Moore, David W., and Sharon Arthur Moore. 1986. "Possible Sentences." In *Reading in the Content Areas: Improving Classroom Instruction.* 2nd edition. Edited by Ernest K. Dishner, Thomas W. Bean, John E. Readence, and David W. Moore. Dubuque, IA: Kendall/Hunt.

Moore, David W., Sharon Arthur Moore, Patricia M. Cunningham, and James W. Cunningham. 1994. *Developing Readers and Writers in the Content Areas K–12.* 2nd edition. White Plains, NY: Longman.

Morrow, Lesley Mandel. 1996. "Collection and Analysis of the Qualitative Data." In *Motivating Reading and Writing in Diverse Classrooms: Social and Physical Contexts in a Literature-Based Program.* Urbana, IL: National Council of Teachers of English.

Nagy, William E. and Judith A. Scott. 2000. "Vocabulary Processes." In *Handbook of Reading Research, Volume III*, edited by Michael L. Kamil and Rebecca Barr. Mahwah, NJ: Lawrence Erlbaum Associates, Inc., 269–284.

National Center for Education Statistics. 2013. "120 Years of Literacy." *National Assessment of Adult Literacy.* http://nces.ed.gov/naal/lit_history.asp.

National Governors Association Center for Best Practices, Council of Chief State School Officers. 2010. *Common Core State Standards: English Language Arts Standards.* Washington, DC: National Governors Association Center for Best Practices, Council of Chief State School Officers.

References Cited *(cont.)*

Ogle, Donna M. 1986. "K-W-L: A teaching model that develops active reading of expository text." *Reading Teacher* 39 (6): 564–70.

Palmatier, Robert A. 1973. "A Notetaking System for Learning." *Journal of Reading* 17 (1): 36–39.

Pauk, Walter. 1988. *A User's Guide to College: Making Notes and Taking Tests*. Lincolnwood, IL: Jamestown Publishers.

Peregoy, Suzanne F., and Owen F. Boyle. 2005. *Reading, Writing, and Learning in ESL: A Resource Book for K–12 Teachers*. 4th Edition. Upper Saddle River, NJ: Pearson Education.

Perkins, Kyle. 1983. "On the Use of Composition Scoring Techniques, Objective Measures, and Objective Tests to Evaluate ESL Writing Ability. *TESOL Quarterly* 17 (4): 651–671.

Pinnell, Gay Su. 1988 (January). "Success of Children at Risk in a Program That Combines Writing and Reading. Technical Report No. 417." In *Reading and Writing Connections*, edited by Jana M. Mason. Boston, MA: Allyn & Bacon.

Pressley, Michael. 1990. *Cognitive Strategy Instruction That Really Improves Children's Academic Performance*. Cambridge, MA: Brookline Books.

Resnick, Lauren B., and Leopold Klopfer, eds. 1989. *Toward the Thinking Curriculum: Current Cognitive Research*. Alexandria, VA: Association for Supervision and Curriculum Development.

Routman, Regie. 2004. *Writing Essentials: Raising Expectations and Results While Simplifying Teaching*. Portsmouth, NH: Heinemann.

Ryder, Randall J. and Michael F. Graves. 2003. *Reading and Learning in Content Areas*. 3rd ed. New York: John Wiley & Sons, Inc.

Santa, Carol Minnick, Lynn Havens, and Shirley Harrison. 1996. "Teaching Secondary Science through Reading, Writing, Studying, and Problem Solving." In *Content Area Reading and Learning: Instructional Strategies*, edited by Diane Lapp, James Flood, and Nancy Farnan. Needham Heights, MA: Allyn & Bacon, 165–179.

Schwartz, Robert M., and Taffy E. Raphael. 1985. "Concept of definition: A key to improving students' vocabulary." *The Reading Teacher* 39 (2): 198–205.

Self, Judy, ed. 1987. *Plain Talk About Learning and Writing Across the Curriculum*. Richmond, VA: Virginia Department of Education.

Sloan, Megan S. 1996. "Encouraging Young Students to Use Interesting Words in Their Writing." *The Reading Teacher* 50 (3): 268–269.

References Cited (cont.)

Smith, Christine C., and Thomas W. Bean. 1980. "The Guided Writing Procedure: Integrating Content Reading and Writing Improvement." *Reading World* 19 (3): 290–294.

Speck, Bruce W. 2002. "Facilitating Students' Collaborative Writing." *ASHE-ERIC Higher Education Report* 28 (6): 8–9.

Staton, Jana. 1980. "Writing and Counseling: Using a Dialogue Journal." *Language Arts* 57 (5): 514–518.

Steffens, H. 1988. "The value and difficulties of teaching the history of science and technology in secondary schools." Paper presented at the Annual Meeting of the American Historical Association. Cincinnati, OH: 17 pages. ED 306 182.

Sullo, Bob. 2007. *Activating the Desire to Learn*. Alexandria, VA: Association for Supervision and Curriculum Development.

Tileston, Donna Walker. 2004. *What Every Educator Should Know About Student Motivation*. Thousand Oaks, CA: Sage.

University of Nebraska-Lincoln Writing Center. 2013. "Assessing Student Writing." *University of Nebraska-Lincoln*. Accessed June 20. http://www.unl.edu/writing/assessing-student-writing.

Van Zile, Susan. 2001. *Awesome Hands-On Activities for Teaching Literacy Elements*. New York: Scholastic, Inc.

Wagner, Tony. 2008. *The Global Acievement Gap*. New York: Basic Books.

Walker, Anne. 1988. "Writing-across-the-Curriculum: The Second Decade." *English Quarterly* 21 (2): 93–103.

Weinstein, Claire E., and Richard E. Mayer. 1986. "The Teaching of Learning Strategies." In *Handbook of Research on Teaching and Learning*, edited by Marlin C. Wittrock. New York: MacMillan, 315–327.

Widmayer, Sharon, Elena Collins, Holly Gray, Laurie Miller, and Gray Rossen. 2004. "Technology that Reaches and Teaches Every Student." TESOL Pre-Convention Institute. Last modified March 27, 2004. http://www.soundsofenglish.org/Presentations/TESOL2004PCI/index.html.

Wolk, Ronald A. 2011. *Wasting Minds: Why Our Education System Is Failing and What We Can Do About It*. Alexandria, VA: Association for Supervision and Curriculum Development.

Worsley, Dale, and Bernadette Mayer, 1989. *The Art of Science Writing*. New York: Teachers and Writers Collaborative.

Yinger, Robert. 1985. "Journal Writing as a Learning Tool." *Volta Review* 87 (5): 21–33.

Cited Literature by Grade Level

Grades 1–2

Berenstain, Jan, and Mike Berenstain. 2009. *The Berenstain Bears' Sick Days*. New York: HarperFestival.

Bradley, Kimberly Brubaker. 2007. *The Perfect Pony*. New York: Dial Books for Young Readers.

Brown, Marc. 1995. *D. W. the Picky Eater*. New York: Little, Brown Books for Young Readers.

Cole, Joanna. 1986–2010. *The Magic School Bus*. New York: Scholastic, Inc.

Henkes, Kevin. 2006. *Lilly's Purple Plastic Purse*. New York: Greenwillow Books.

Lobel, Arnold. 1976. *Frog and Toad All Year*. New York: HarperCollins.

McCloskey, Robert. 1952. *One Morning in Maine*. New York: Viking Penguin.

McCloskey, Robert. 1969. *Make Way for Ducklings*. New York: The Viking Press.

Osborne, Mary Pope. 1992. *Dinosaurs Before Dark*. New York: Random House Books for Young Readers.

Waddell, Martin. 1996. *Owl Babies*. Somerville, MA: Candlewick Press.

Zion, Gene. 1984. *Harry the Dirty Dog*. New York: HarperTrophy.

Grades 3–5

Allard, Harry. 1977. *Miss Nelson Is Missing!* New York: Houghton Mifflin.

Blume, Judy. 1971. *Freckle Juice*. New York: Simon & Schuster Books for Young Readers.

Brown, Marcia. 1947. *Stone Soup*. New York: Aladdin Paperbacks.

Burnett, Frances Hodgson. 1951. *The Secret Garden*. New York: Puffin Books.

Burnett, Frances Hodgson. 1994. *A Little Princess*. New York: Random House Books for Young Readers.

Cannon, Janell. 1997. *Stellaluna*. New York: HMH Books for Young Readers.

Cannon, Janell. 2005. *Crickwing*. New York: HMH Books for Young Readers.

Cleary, Beverly. 1955. *Beezus and Ramona*. New York: Avon Books.

Cleary, Beverly. 1982. *Ralph S. Mouse*. New York: HarperCollins.

Curtis, Christopher Paul. 1995. *The Watsons Go to Birmingham—1963*. New York: Yearling.

Dahl, Roald. 1964. *The Magic Finger*. New York: Puffin Books.

Hoban, Russell. 1960. *Bedtime for Frances*. New York: HarperCollins Children's Books.

Cited Literature by Grade Level *(cont.)*

Lindgren, Astrid. 1950. *Pippi Longstocking.* New York: The Viking Press.

MacLachlan, Patricia. 1996. *Sarah, Plain and Tall.* New York: Scholastic, Inc.

Smith, Robert Kimmel. 1972. *Chocolate Fever.* New York: Coward, McCann & Geoghegan.

Spyri, Johanna. 1956. *Heidi.* New York: Puffin Books.

White, E. B. 1952. *Charlotte's Web.* New York: HarperTrophy.

White, E. B. 1945. *Stuart Little.* New York: HarperTrophy.

Wilder, Laura Ingalls. 1932. *Little House in the Big Woods.* New York: HarperCollins.

Grades 6–8

Alcott, Louisa May. 1983. *Little Women.* New York: Bantam Dell.

Avi [pseud.]. 1990. *The True Confessions of Charlotte Doyle.* New York: Scholastic, Inc.

Babbitt, Natalie. 1975. *Tuck Everlasting.* New York: Square Fish.

Balliet, Blue. 2012. *Chasing Vermeer.* New York: Scholastic.

Bulla, Clyde Robert. 1981. *A Lion to Guard Us.* New York: HarperCollins.

Burnett, Frances Hodgson. 1951. *The Secret Garden.* New York: Puffin Books.

Carroll, Lewis. 1993. *Alice's Adventures in Wonderland.* Mineola, NY: Dover Publications.

Catling, Patrick Skene. 1952. *The Chocolate Touch.* New York: Bantam Books, Inc.

Cushman, Karen. 2012. *The Midwife's Apprentice.* New York: Houghton Mifflin Harcourt.

Dahl, Roald. 1961. *James and the Giant Peach.* New York: Bantam Books, Inc.

Golding, William. 1954. *Lord of the Flies.* New York: Penguin Putnam.

Levine, Gail Carson. 1997. *Ella Enchanted.* New York: HarperCollins.

Palacio, R. J. 2012. *Wonder.* New York: Alfred A. Knopf.

Paulsen, Gary. 1996. *Hatchet.* New York: First Aladdin Paperbacks.

Peck, Robert Newton. 1972. *A Day No Pigs Would Die.* New York: Laurel-Leaf.

Raskin, Ellen. 2004. *The Westing Game.* New York: Puffin Modern Classics.

Rawls, Wilson. 1997. *Where the Red Fern Grows.* New York: Scholastic, Inc.

Riordan, Rick. *Rick Riordan's Heroes of Olympus Series Three Book Set.* New York: Hyperion.

Rowling, J. K. 1997–2007. *Harry Potter.* New York: Scholastic, Inc.

Cited Literature by Grade Level (cont.)

Scott, Michael. 2007. *The Alchemyst: The Secrets of the Immortal Nicholas Flamel*. New York: Delacorte Press.

Shelley, Mary. 2000. *Frankenstein*. Boston, MA: Bedford/St. Martin's.

Steinbeck, John. 1938. *Of Mice and Men*. New York: The Viking Press.

Vanderpool, Clare. 2010. *Moon Over Manifest*. New York: Yearling.

Grades 9–12

Achebe, Chinua. 1996. *Things Fall Apart*. Portsmouth, NH: Heinemann.

Agee, James. 2008. *A Death in the Family*. New York: Penguin Books.

Austen, Jane. 1995. *Pride and Prejudice*. Mineola, NY: Dover Publications.

Bradbury, Ray. 1950. *Fahrenheit 451*. New York: Ballantine Books.

Brontë, Emily. 1996. *Wuthering Heights*. Mineola, NY: Dover Publications.

Brontë, Emily. 2008. *Jane Eyre*. Radford, VA: Wilder Publications.

Cather, Willa. 1994. *My Ántonia*. Mineola, NY: Dover Publications.

Cisneros, Sandra. 1984. *The House on Mango Street*. New York: Vintage Books.

Collins, Suzanne. 2010. *The Hunger Games*. New York: Scholastic.

Conrad, Joseph. 1990. *Heart of Darkness*. Mineola, NY: Dover Publications.

Fitzgerald, F. Scott. 2004. *The Great Gatsby*. New York: Scribner.

Gaines, Ernest J. 1993. *A Lesson Before Dying*. New York: Vintage Books.

Hemingway, Ernest. 2012. *A Farewell to Arms*. New York: Scribner.

Hoskins, Esther Forbes. 1943. *Johnny Tremain*. New York: Houghton Mifflin Harcourt Publishing Company.

Kingsolver, Barbara. 1988. *The Bean Trees*. New York: HarperCollins.

O'Brien, Tim. 1990. *The Things They Carried*. New York: Houghton Mifflin Harcourt Publishing Company.

Shakespeare, William. 2007. *A Midsummer Night's Dream*, edited by Mario Digangi. New York: Barnes & Noble.

Steinbeck, John. 1939. *The Grapes of Wrath*. New York: The Viking Press.

Tan, Amy. 1991. *The Kitchen God's Wife*. New York: Penguin Books.

Zusak, Markus. 2005. *The Book Thief*. New York: Alfred A. Knopf.

Contents of the Digital Resource CD

Pages	Resource	Filename
29	Correlation to Standards	standards.pdf
41	Frayer Model	frayermodel.pdf frayermodel.doc
50	Word Trails	wordtrails.pdf wordtrails.doc
55	Word Questioning	wordquestioning.pdf wordquestioning.doc
60	Open Word Sort	wordsort.pdf wordsort.doc
68	Think Sheet	thinksheet.pdf thinksheet.doc
72	Free-Association Brainstorming	freeassociation.pdf freeassociation.doc
83	Reader-Response Writing Chart	readerresponse.pdf readerresponse.doc
88	Story Impressions	storyimpressions.pdf storyimpressions.doc
93	Story Prediction Chart	predictionchart.pdf predictionchart.doc
113	Double-Entry Journal	doubleentry.pdf doubleentry.doc
117	Questioning Journal	questioning.pdf questioning.doc
122	Cornell Note-Taking System	cornellsystem.pdf cornellsystem.doc
126	Note-Taking System for Learning	notesystemlearning.pdf notesystemlearning.doc
129	T-List	tlist.pdf tlist.doc
140	Frame	frame.pdf frame.doc
144	Venn Diagram	venndiagram.pdf venndiagram.doc
148	Conflict-Resolution Map	conflictresolution.pdf conflictresolution.doc

Contents of the Digital Resource CD *(cont.)*

Pages	Resource	Filename
152	Semantic Word Map	semanticwordmap.pdf
156	Story Strip	storystrip.pdf storystrip.doc
161	Plot Diagram	plotdiagram.pdf plotdiagram.doc
173	Read, Encode, Annotate, Ponder	reap.pdf reap.doc
185	GIST	gist.pdf gist.doc
192	Guided Reading and Summarizing Procedure	grasp.pdf grasp.doc
198	Character Summary	charactersummary.pdf charactersummary.doc
204	Story Mapping	storymapping.pdf storymapping.doc
209	Summary-Writing Microtheme	summarywriting.pdf summarywriting.doc
211	RAFT Assignment	raft.pdf raft.doc
213	Formal Letter	formalletter.pdf formalletter.doc
215	Friendly Letter	friendlyletter.pdf friendlyletter.doc
217	Newspaper Article	newspaperarticle.pdf newspaperarticle.doc
219	Historical/Science Fiction Story	historicalscience.pdf historicalscience.doc
221	Character Diary	characterdiary.pdf characterdiary.doc
223	Story Additions	storyadditions.pdf storyadditions.doc
228	Holistic Assessment	holistic.pdf holistic.doc
230	Analytic Assessment	analytic.pdf analytic.doc
232	Primary Trait Assessment	primarytrait.pdf primarytrait.doc